Sport Teams, Fans, and Twitter

INTEGRATED MARKETING COMMUNICATION

Series Editor: Jeanne M. Persuit
University of North Carolina Wilmington

Integrated marketing communication (IMC) is a holistic approach to the areas of advertising, public relations, branding, promotions, event and experiential marketing, and related fields of strategic communication. This series seeks to ground IMC with communication ethics in order to take the theory and practice of IMC beyond a critical and deconstructive understanding and into new areas of productive inquiry. We seek to advance the scholarship of IMC in a manner that influences and informs future practice. Submissions may rely on varied methodologies and relate to the study and practice of communication and its theoretical diversity, including but not limited to the areas of rhetoric, visual communication, media ecology, philosophy of communication, mass communication, intercultural communication, and instructional communication. We welcome submissions addressing all facets of IMC and its relationship with communication ethics. While edited volumes will be considered, we encourage the submission of scholarly monographs that explore, in-depth, issues in IMC as related to communication ethics.

Titles in the series:

Sport Teams, Fans, and Twitter: The Influence of Social Media on Relationships and Branding
By Brandi Watkins

Integrated Marketing Communication: Creating Spaces for Engagement
Edited by Jeanne M. Persuit and Christina L. McDowell Marinchak

Sport Teams, Fans, and Twitter

The Influence of Social Media on Relationships and Branding

Brandi Watkins

LEXINGTON BOOKS

Lanham • Boulder • New York • London

Published by Lexington Books
An imprint of The Rowman & Littlefield Publishing Group, Inc.
4501 Forbes Boulevard, Suite 200, Lanham, Maryland 20706
www.rowman.com

6 Tinworth Street, London SE11 5AL, United Kingdom

British Library Cataloguing in Publication Information Available

Library of Congress Cataloging-in-Publication Data
ISBN 978-1-4985-4005-6 (cloth : alk. paper)
ISBN 978-1-4985-4007-0 (paperback : alk. paper)
ISBN 978-1-4985-4006-3 (electronic)

Contents

Part One

TWITTER FOR
RELATIONSHIP BUILDING

Do you remember where you were in October of 2004 when the Boston Red Sox defeated the St. Louis Cardinals and the Curse of the Bambino to win the Major League Baseball (MLB) World Series? How about in 2016 when after a rain delay and extra innings, the Chicago Cubs won their first World Series ending their seventy-one-year championship drought? In 1980 the U.S. Men's Hockey team made history when they defeated the Soviets, who had won the gold medal in the previous four Olympic Games. A crowd of about 10,000 people were in attendance for the "Miracle on Ice" game, but as the legend of the game grew, so did the crowd size.

The legends and myths of sport heroes are stories woven into the fabric of who we are as people. For me, I have two vivid sport memories that solidified my love of sports. The first was during the 1996 Olympics in Atlanta. I have always loved watching women's gymnastics. I was a clumsy and uncoordinated kid, but gymnasts on the other hand, were the epitome of strength and grace. I loved watching the floor routine. The combination of precision dancing and tumbling along with the personality of the gymnasts was everything I wished I could do and be. In 1996 the U.S. women's gymnastics team, dubbed "The Magnificent Seven," became the first team to win the gold medal for the United States. What I remember most about that performance was the vault by Kerri Strug, who stuck the landing on her second vault after sustaining an ankle injury. I remember watching Strug's coach carry her back to the bench after the vault. I remember watching the medal ceremony and hearing the national anthem play with pride, knowing I just watched something special.

The second sport memory that left a lasting impression on me came a year later during the 1997 National Basketball Association (NBA) finals. My love for basketball and the NBA was solidified in the mid-1990s. I missed out on the Magic Johnson and Larry Bird era, but I grew up with Michael Jordan, the greatest of all time. My favorite time to watch basketball was the playoffs. The NBA playoffs meant it was summer. It meant the days were longer and my bedtime was later. And at that time, it meant watching more epic battles between Michael Jordan and whoever his foe was that year—whether it was the Phoenix Suns led by Charles Barkley or Gary Payton and the Seattle Super Sonics or the Utah Jazz led by John Stockton and Karl Malone.

Despite this era of great basketball, the game that stands out to me the most is Jordan's flu game. It was Game Five of the 1997 Finals and the series between the Chicago Bulls and the Utah Jazz was tied 2–2. The game was played in Salt Lake City. Jordan was exhibiting severe flu-like symptoms and was dehydrated for most of the game. The Bulls were trailing the Jazz in the fourth quarter when with thirty seconds left in the game Jordan hit a three that gave the Bulls the lead and eventually the game. The Bulls would go on to win the series and the championship in Game Six. The indelible image of this game was watching Scottie Pippen help carry an exhausted Jordan off the court.

These stories exemplify what makes sports important. Stories of greatness and heroism. Stories of overcoming obstacles and defeating the odds to be the best. Sports are important because they transcend the monotony of everyday life. The significance of sport dates back to the Industrial Revolution, when people left their homes and families seeking work in factories in larger cities. Urbanization brought about financial opportunities, but it also brought about intense isolation and loneliness. During this time, leaving home was not commonplace and so to cope, people turned to sports. Local sport leagues in cities provided people with an outlet to escape their current situation to find companionship and belonging in a new place (Pedersen, Miloch, and Laucella 2007).

This holds true today. Sports still help bring people together, and as globalization increases and more people leave their homes and country in search of opportunity, sports are still an important component of keeping us connected. Look no further than the increasing popularity of international sports like the World Cup and the Olympics. A few years ago, I was fortunate to teach a study abroad class about the influence of the Olympics. Over the course of our two weeks in Switzerland, fourteen students from diverse backgrounds were able to connect with one another over their shared memories of the Olympics. As part of the trip, we visited the Olympic Museum in Lausanne where we took in all of the artifacts of a sporting event that brings the world together and allows us to learn about ourselves and other cultures.

Sport fandom can enhance feelings of connectedness to the larger community. Sport fans do not think of the team and the community as separate entities but rather view them as being inextricably linked, which can enhance civic pride (Heere and James 2007). April 27, 2011, an EF4 tornado ravaged a six-mile swatch of Tuscaloosa, Alabama, a place best known for its storied football team the University of Alabama Crimson Tide. In the aftermath of the storm that took the lives of forty-one people, six of whom were students at the university, the community rallied around its beloved football team for a welcome distraction from the long rebuilding process. Head Football Coach Nick Saban said, "We can create a psychological escape for the people of this town. They have a great passion for sports, and we'll be there for them" (Anderson 2011). The following year (2012) teams from the University of Alabama won national championships in football, women's softball, women's golf, and women's gymnastics.

Sports provides a unique lens for how we see the world, others, and ourselves. In a Birmingham, Alabama, Ted Talk, Dr. Andrew Billings, a sport communication scholar, said the following:

> Sports have power; therefore, we need to teach sports. Not how to play them, I think we have that covered, but how to consume them and how to understand them . . . how to talk about them. Because when we teach sports, we often teach those larger issues as well—gender, domestic violence, religion, identity (TedxTalk 2014)

The reason why sports have power, the reason why sports are important, can be attributed to one key concept—the relationship between sports teams and sports fans. Brand relationships are a mutually beneficial relationship where both parties find value.

SOCIAL MEDIA AND SPORTS

In recent years, social media sites have transitioned from being a place to connect with family and friends to include organizations and brands. Since social media was first developed as a networking tool for interpersonal relationships, using social media required brands to think beyond traditional one-way advertising and marketing techniques to sell products and services. Instead, to use social media effectively, brands have to use the platforms the same way as everyone else—to connect and build relationships with others. Over the last five years, brands have become more sophisticated in how they use social media as a marketing tool that goes beyond pushing a sale, but instead focuses on relationship building with consumers.

As social media has become more integrated into strategic communication efforts, practitioners and scholars alike have touted the benefits of social media. The personalized nature of communication on social media and the interactive capabilities of the platforms means that brands can increase brand awareness and make great strides in terms of developing meaningful relationships with consumers. What distinguishes social media from other forms of media commonly used in strategic communication, is the capability for immediate two-way communication. The capability for immediate two-way communication is what distinguishes social media from other forms of media. This immediacy allows brands to attend to the consumers' needs in a more expedited manner, which is crucial for the development of positive consumer-brand relationships. It is positive online experiences with brands that can lead to the formation of continued online relationships (Morgan-Thomas and Veloutsou 2013).

To fully utilize the attributes of social media as a marketing tool, brands need to focus more on the relational aspects of marketing. As such, relationship marketing is an often-cited strategy for effectively using social media as a marketing tool. Relationship marketing strategies emphasize building long-term relationships with consumers, rather than one-time transactions. There are three elements necessary to carry out a relationship marketing plan: (1) seek direct contact with consumers, (2) build a database of consumer information, and (3) develop a customer-oriented service system (Groonroos 1994, 5). With the advent of social media, these elements can be carried out online. Social media allows brand to have direct contact with consumers without having to go through the media filter as in traditional marketing tactics. The act of following and networking that occurs between brands and consumers allow for the creation of a database-type list of consumers, and the two-way capability of social media allows for interaction between the brand and the consumer. Furthermore, social media can be used to provide unique, personalized messages to consumers (Simmons 2007; Meng, Stavros, and Westberg 2015), encourage dialogue between the brand and the consumer (Stavros et al. 2014), and create brand communities of loyal brand enthusiasts (Hedlund 2014; Meng, Stavros, and Westberg 2015).

BOOK OVERVIEW

Sport Teams, Fans, and Twitter is about the fan-team relationship and how social media, specifically the microblogging site Twitter, can be used to enhance and maintain the fan-team relationship. The commitment of sport fans to the team is a crucial aspect to the success of the sport brand, and as such sport brands need to develop communication strategies that promote lasting fan-team relationships. Sport brands that are able to master the dynamics of social media to establish a strong presence are better equipped to garner consumer attention, increase brand awareness, and maintain communication with consumers (Kwon and Sung 2011). One strategy for developing fan-team relationship is to utilize Twitter as a relationship-building tool. The rationale for focusing on Twitter will be explained in chapter 2.

The research presented in this book is guided by two goals—(1) provide empirical support online fan engagement on Twitter as an effective relationship-building tool and (2) to examine the content strategies produced by professional sport teams. A mixed methods approach was used to accomplish these research goals. Self-identified sport fans who use Twitter to follow sports were surveyed to assess their perception of the fan-team relationship and how they engage with their favorite team on Twitter. Findings from the survey, presented in chapter 3, provide empirical support for online engagement on Twitter to have a positive influence on the fan-team relationship. Then, a thematic analysis of tweets produced by professional sport teams was conducted to better understand content strategies teams produced as part of its relationship marketing efforts. Taken together, these two goals provide a comprehensive examination of the effectiveness of online engagement and strategies used to enhance the fan-team relationship.

Part I of this book relates to the first research goal. chapter 1 provides the background information on the nature of sport fandom and the sport brand that necessitates strong fan-team relationships. Chapter 2 addresses why social media, and Twitter in particular, are useful tools for facilitating fan-team relationship-building efforts. Results of the survey research is presented in chapter 3.

Part II of the book addresses the second research goal—to analyze content strategies implemented by professional sport teams on Twitter. Chapters 4 through 6 present findings from this research. Drawing on research and theory in brand personality, interacting with professional athletes, and dialogue, a thematic analysis provides a typology of the types of content fans encounter from their favorite teams on Twitter. Chapter 7 concludes the book with research-based recommendations for practitioners and scholars.

Chapter 1

The Fan-Team Relationship

For as long as I can remember, the Dallas Cowboys has been a part of my family. Every Thanksgiving, the Cowboys were there as we ate turkey and dressing. If there were plans for a Sunday afternoon in the fall, they had to end in time to get home to catch the Cowboy's game. My earliest memories of the Super Bowl include the Cowboys and their three championships in the 1990s. My family's relationship with the Cowboys started with my dad, who grew up in the 1970s idolizing Roger Staubach and America's Team. My dad passed his affinity for the Cowboys down to my brother (I was always more of an NBA fan), who at ten years old wrote a fan letter to quarterback Troy Aikman and received an autographed photo of his sport hero. Now, my brother has a son and when he gets older, he will watch the Cowboys play with his dad and the Cowboys will remain a part of our family for the next generation.

Our story is similar to that of other families; sport fandom is often a family affair passed down through generations. Affinity and fandom for collegiate athletics is another example of how sport fandom can be passed down through families. Younger generations want to follow in the footsteps of their parents or older siblings and have the same collegiate experience. I see this a lot working at a university with a noteworthy athletic program. I ask students what made them choose this university, and I almost always get answers like "I went to football games here when I was a kid" or "my family loves the sports program." What these stories illustrate is the longevity of sport fandom, which is an important component of fan-team relationships.

In order to understand the fan-team relationship, it is necessary to look at both parties—the fan perspective and the team perspective.

THE FAN PERSPECTIVE

For many, sport fandom allows them to become part of a group that transcends the routine of daily life (Branscombe and Wann 1991). As such, sports go beyond the on-field competition and allow fans to "live the brand at different moments of their daily lives" (Couvelaere and Richelieu 2005, 25). Sport fans tend to be highly identified and involved with their favorite team (Underwood, Bond, and Baer 2001) and are more likely to engage in behaviors that promote the team including wearing team-licensed merchandise, attending games, and using social media to follow the team. To understand what drives sport fan behaviors requires understanding social identification theory.

Social Identification Theory

Social identification theory provides a foundation for better understanding how one becomes part of and involved with a group. In order to better understand social identification theory, it is necessary to take a step back and look at the concept of identification. Identification is the perception of oneness with an organization or social group, which is a collection of individuals who share a common bond and pronounce themselves as members of the same group (Ashforth and Mael 1989; Bergami and Bagozzi, 2000; Stets and Burke 2000; Tajfel 1982). Identification is the process that enables social identification to occur. There are two components necessary to achieve identification: (1) a cognitive awareness of group membership and (2) an evaluative component in which the awareness is related to group values (Tajfel 1982, 2). One achieves identification with a social group through acknowledgement of group affiliation (Bergami and Bagozzi 2000). This does not necessarily mean that a person must interact with or be involved with the group. The perception of being a member of the group often satisfies the need for affiliation even in the absence of physical and interpersonal interactions (Ashforth and Mael 1989). Second, as it relates to group values, the person must analyze the group to determine if they perceive their values to align with those of the group.

   As previously mentioned, identification with an organization is what allows for the process of social identification to occur. The underlying assumption of social identity theory is that a person has both a personal identity and a social identity. A personal identity includes individual-specific attributes that define a person, including talents and interests. Social identity, on the other hand, is a person's public image manifest through group memberships (Fink et al. 2009). In other words, personal identity is defined by individual-specific attributes, and social identity is defined by group memberships. Tajfel (1982, 24) defines social identity as "that part of the individuals' self-concept which derives from their knowledge of their membership of a social group (or groups) together with the value and emotional significance of that membership." According to social identity theory, a person defines their social identity in terms of group membership. The greater the emotional connection a person has with the group, then the more significant that group membership becomes to their overall identity.

Social identification is important because it is how we make sense of the social world. According to social identity theory, social groups are an important component of organizing and simplifying a complex world (Ashforth and Mael 1989; Trepte 2006). Part of the process of identification includes self-categorizing into social groups. Self-categorization is the process of organizing individuals into social categories or groups (Ellemers and Haslam 2011), which helps us define ourselves and others (Carlson and Donavan 2008; Donavan, Carlson, and Zimmerman 2005). Through this classification system, a person is able to locate and define themselves in terms of the social environment (Ashforth and Mael 1989) and make sense of the world (Trepte 2006).

Social identity theory positions the individual as an active participant in creating his or her public persona through identification with social groups (Underwood, Bond, and Baer 2001; Lock et al. 2012). It is the self-definitional aspect of group memberships that is the centerpiece of social identity theory. According to social identity theory, individuals choose to identify with an organization when they feel a sense of belonging, are able to categorize into in-group and out-group status, and adopt similar attitudes and beliefs in group settings (Ashforth and Mael 1989; Tajfel 1982; Tajfel and Turner 2004). Social identity is derived from group memberships, and people navigate through these group memberships to maintain a positive social identity (Brown 2000). As a person identifies with an organization, they begin to incorporate the organization into their own self-definition (Fink, Trail, and Anderson 2002). The same concept can be applied to sport. As a person identifies with a sport team, then the more likely they are to incorporate the team into their identity.

A person can be a member of multiple social groups (Hogg, Terry, and White 1995), but the emotional connection and sense of belonging varies from group to group (Tajfel 1982). As such, the social group where an individual feels a sense of belonging becomes a self-defining feature for an individual (Hogg, Terry, and White 1995) and influences how they perceive and interpret events (Hogg, Terry, and White 1995; Underwood, Bond, and Baer 2001). Highly identified group members tend to adopt beliefs and behaviors of the group and are motivated to maintain these actions to ensure group membership (Christian, Bagozzi, Abrams, and Rosenthal 2012). The enhanced importance of group identification leads to a heightened sense of in-group and out-group classifications. The in-group is defined as others who are categorized with the self and share a common social identification and out-group as people who do not identify with the in-group (Stets and Burke 2000). As the differences between the in-group and out-group become more salient, an individual sees him or herself as an "exemplar of their social group" and are motivated to maintain a positive self-concept through group membership and intergroup comparisons (Bergami and Bagozzi 2000; Phua 2010). It is at this point that group membership is internalized to the point that it contributes to a person's sense of self (Haslam and Ellemers 2005). This internalization of group membership is what ultimately leads to sport fandom.

Sport Fandom

Fan identification is an expression of social identity theory. Fan identification is defined as a "personal commitment and emotional involvement customers have with a sports organization, incorporating both psychological and behavioral aspects of identification" (Underwood, Bond, and Baer 2001, 3). Likewise, sport team identification is defined as "the extent to which individuals perceive themselves as fans of the team, are involved with the team, are concerned with the team's performance, and *view the team as a representation of themselves*" (Branscombe and Wann 1992, 1017, emphasis added). Fan identification and team identification have been used interchangeably in the literature because both concepts center on the notion of identification with a group, which creates a feeling of solidarity, and an "us versus them" mentality (Phua 2010). Identification with a sport team also incites higher levels of optimism about team performance among fans (Heere and James 2007).

The sense of belonging that sport fans experience becomes a defining point in a person's social identity (Karjaluoto, Munnukka, and Salmi 2016). Sport fans consider themselves to be members of the organization, not merely spectators or consumers of the product (Heere and James 2007). In other words, "when highly identified fans show support for their team a sense of togetherness can diffuse through the group via sharing of deeply held interests and familiar identities" (Stavros et al. 2014, 457). This feeling of group membership is strengthened by the connection and emotional involvement a fan has with his or her favorite team to the point that the team's victories and failures are experienced on a deeply personal level (Madrigal and Chen 2008; Stevens and Rosenberger 2012).

Motivations for Sport Fandom

There is not one single factor that precipitates sport fandom, but rather fandom is influenced by a variety of experiences, attitudes, and opinions about the team (Stavros et al. 2014). Wann (1995) was among the first to propose a set of motivations for sport fandom, including eustress, aesthetic pleasure, escape, entertainment, family needs, group affiliation, economic gain, and self-esteem (also cited in Stavros et al. 2014). Other factors contributing to the development of fan identification include geographical location, team success, and ability to attend games (Funk and James 2006), family or friend connections to a team (Havard 2014), and internal factors (e.g., demographic and psychographic information) and external factors (e.g., team culture and location; Kunkel, Doyle, and Funk 2014).

From a psychological perspective, those who present high levels of team identification and fandom tend to have a favorable attitude toward the team that reflects their core attitudes, values, self-concept, information processing, and behavior, which in turn, allows for an even stronger commitment to the team (Funk and James 2001). In other words, when a sport team exhibits behavior that is consistent with a fan's core attitudes and values, then identification with a team becomes an even more significant component of a person's identity. Furthermore, behaviors associated with fandom and team identification explains loyalty to a sport team despite losing seasons (Dwyer, Greenhalgh, and LeCrom 2015).

Sport Fan Involvement

The concept of involvement is also important for understanding fandom. Involvement is "an internal state variable that reflects the amount of arousal, interest, or drive evoked by a particular stimuli or situation that mediates consumer behavior" (Funk, Ridinger, and Mooreman 2004, 36). A person is considered to be a fan when involvement with the team becomes a central and meaningful activity in a person's life (Stevens and Rosenberger 2012). Being a fan is a continual searching process, where the fan desires to seek out information about the team on a regular basis even during the off-season. The more identified and involved a fan is with a team, the more likely they are to seek out information about the team and find ways to publicly display identification with the team.

Not all sport fans are highly identified with a team or display passionate allegiance to the team (Stewart, Smith, and Nicholson 2003). Sport researchers typically assess fandom on a continuum based on a person's interest in sport with low-identified spectators on one end and high-identified and involved fans on the other end (Funk and James 2001; Underwood, Bond, and Baer

2001). Spectators and fans use sport to meet a variety of psychological, social, and emotional needs (Stewart, Smith, and Nicholson 2003). For some fans, involvement with the team is a self-defining characteristic, while for others it is a way to socialize and pass time.

A commonly used typology for sport fans addresses these motivations. According to this typology there are three broad categories of sport fans: (1) social fans, (2) focused fans, and (3) vested fans (Sutton et al. 1997). Social fans have a more limited sense of identification with a team and mainly consume sport for social benefits. The focused fan represents a more moderate level of identification, and the vested fan is considered to be a die-hard fan and represents the highest level of identification. As the motivation for consuming sports differs among these three groups, so does the level of engagement with a sport brand. In other words, a sport brand should not expect high levels of engagement among all consumers all of the time. There may, in fact, only be a small contingent of consumers who are willing to go to such lengths to engage with a brand. However, as it is those consumers who are going to exhibit more brand loyalty and be more open to engaging in a relationship with the brand (Malthouse et al. 2016).

Evaluating Sport Fandom

Sport researchers have worked to develop models to explain the varying degrees of sport fandom. In one instance, three tiers of sport fans are proposed: (1) those with an emotional connection to the team, these are fans considered to be highly identified and incorporate team identification as a defining characteristics of their social identification; (2) fans who are considered to be moderately identified with the team, who mainly seek out sport to meet excitement and entertainment needs, and identification with the team is moderately important; and (3) fans with lower levels of fan identification teams use sport as a mechanism for social interaction and entertainment, identification with a team is least important for these fans (Stewart, Smith, and Nicholson 2003).

The psychological continuum model (PCM), introduced by Funk and James (2001), was developed to better understand the distinction between sport spectators and fans through examination of psychological connections to sport. According to the PCM, a person moves through four phases when developing a connection to the team that leads to fandom: (1) awareness of the sport or team, (2) attraction to the team or sport, (3) attachment to a specific team through identifying a team as a favorite, and (4) allegiance to a specific team through becoming a loyal and committed fan of the team. Distinguishing between levels of sport fan involvement is important for sport brands. Each group has a different motivation for consuming sport and developing specialized branding and marketing messages to meet the needs of fans can further enhance the fan-team relationship, which as will be discussed later is an essential component for the success of the organization.

Sport consumption is about more than watching a game and going on about one's life (Stewart, Smith, and Nicholson 2003). Identification with a sport team can lead to increased self-esteem through "linking their knowledge and emotions with their team's performance" (Stavros et al. 2014, 457). For sport fans, knowing intimate information about the team, including traditions and rituals, is an important aspect of socializing with other fans within the group (Hedlund 2014). Additionally, sport fans can have an enhanced feeling of personal satisfaction and achievement through the team's success (Havard 2014), and the feeling of belonging to a group of sport fans satisfies the need for social belonging (Heere and James 2007; Wann 1995). The feeling of acceptance and involvement with other fans opens the door to engaging in activities that are beneficial to the brand, including attending games and team-sponsored events and engaging with the team online (Karjaluoto, Munnukka, and Salmi 2016). Furthermore, participation in team rituals and traditions reinforce the feeling of belonging among the fan community (Hedlund 2014).

THE TEAM PERSPECTIVE

Sports are a business, and a very profitable one at that. According to Forbes, there are at least eighty-six sport franchises worth $1 billion (Badenhausen 2017). Among those, the Dallas Cowboys ($4.2 billion), New York Yankees ($3.7 billion), and Manchester United ($3.69 billion) are the most valuable sport brands (Badenhausen 2017). Given the economic impact of the sport industry, many sports organizations, including professional sport teams, have taken on operating practices similar to other business industries including strategic communications and human resources (Hopwood 2005). Beyond economic impact, the sport industry plays an important role in the cultural and political arenas as well (L'Etang 2006). Thus, sports are about more than a team playing a game. Sports are, in most cases, successful brands.

Sport Teams as Brands

A brand is defined as "a name, term, sign, symbol, or design or combination of them which is intended to identify the goods and services of one seller or a group of sellers and to differentiate them from those of competitors" (Keller 1993, 2). A strong brand has components that are easily identifiable, make a lasting impact on the consumer, and provide a sense of meaning and value for the consumer (Wallace, Wilson, and Miloch 2011). An effective brand provides information to the consumer; therefore, simplifying the time-consuming process of searching and comparing products and services from other competitors (Simmons 2007). The previous definition provides a basic understanding of what a brand is, but in order to better understand why relationships are important for sport brands, it is important to go one step further and distinguish between the product-based brand and the service brand and determine where sport fits within those sectors.

Brands are divided into two broad categories—product-based brands and service-based brands. A product-based brand sells an actual product to the consumer. For product-based brands, the tangible product purchased by the consumer serves as the signifier of the brand (Berry 2000). Marketing of product-based brands is largely transactional; a consumer pays for the good that is provided by the organization. The consumer walks away with a product that signifies the transaction. The value of the product-based brand is defined largely by the quality of the product produced. Service-based brands, on the other hand, are a little more complicated. Service-based brands do not have a tangible product, but rather the consumer pays for a service that is carried out by the organization. For example, going to a salon for a haircut is an example of a service. When you pay a stylist for a haircut, you are paying for their expertise, not a tangible product. This distinction is important for understanding the implications for branding and marketing service-based brands.

Sport Teams as Service-Based Brands

Consuming the sport product, a game, is akin to consuming a service. Thus, sports are classified as a service-based brand (Underwood, Bond, and Baer 2001). There are four identifying characteristics of service-based brands: (1) intangibility, (2) heterogeneity, (3) inseparability, and (4) perishability (de Chernatony and Riley 1999; Ross 2006; Sheth 2002; Tsai 2011). The intangibility characteristic refers to the lack of a physical packaged good exchanged between the consumer and brand during purchase. The emphasis on the service experience means that the nature of the interaction is heterogeneous, or interactions between the consumer and the organization are individualized and different. Inseparability refers to the simultaneous production and consumption of the service. Finally, services occur on an individual basis and thus are unable to be stored for later consumption.

Sport brands are characterized as a service-based brands, as many of the characteristics of the sport product (i.e., watching a game) align with the characteristics of service brands. A consumer watches the game as it is played resulting in simultaneous production and consumption, thus meeting the inseparability requirement (Ross 2006). Since the product is created and consumed simultaneously, the consumer does not have an opportunity to evaluate the quality prior to purchase, which exemplifies the intangibility requirement. The sport consumption experience is fleeting due to its "intangible, inconsistent, and perishable nature" (Gladden, Milne, and Sutton 1998, 5) thereby making the consumption of a sporting event a one-time transaction, making this a perishable transaction. Due to the limitations of service-based brands, the brand must maintain service consistent with quality (Ross 2006). The sport brand itself plays an integral role in defining the quality of service.

Service-based brands do not have a label, product, or package to display as a result of the brand experience, which indicates that "branding plays a special role in the service companies because strong brands increase customers' trust of the invisible purchase" (Berry 2000, 128). In other words, branding is essential for marketing service-based brands due to the intangible nature of the service brand (Berry 2000; Underwood, Bond, and Baer 2001). A strong brand for service marketers is conceptualized as "what the organization says the brand is, what others say, and how the organization performs the service—all from the customer's point of view," (Ross, James, and Vargas 2006, 261). For service-based brands, the organization is the brand and the brand acts as a promise of future satisfaction for the consumer (Aggarwal 2004; Berry 2000). In the sport context, this means that the team and those who represent the team (e.g., players, coaches, executives, etc.) make up the team brand, and the team's brand is largely determined by the experience that fans have with the team whether it is winning games, celebrating a franchise's storied history, or creating a unique game-watching experience.

Service-based brands operate in a homogenous market where each organization is producing essentially the same service. Strong branding that differentiates the service from others and provides the consumer with a point of distinction in making purchase decisions (Aggarwal 2004; Berry 2000). Like other service-based brands, sport brands operate in a homogenous marketplace. In the United States, professional sports are divided into sport leagues (e.g., Major League Baseball, National Basketball Association, National Football League, National Hockey League, etc.), and those leagues are made up of teams. The teams in each of these leagues provide the same basic service—a competitive sporting event. Therefore, teams must create unique brand associations and personalities that help to differentiate the brand, which provide the intangible qualities associated with that brand that are important for creating brand value.

Consumers and Service-Based Brands

For service-based brands, consumers play an important role in determining the value of service-based brands, which means the goal of service-based branding should be to provide a service that is important and valuable to the consumer (Berry 2000). The sport brand consists of a series of perceptions and experiences sport consumers (e.g., fans) have with the brand. One of the key qualities of sport that establish it as a service brand is the level of involvement of the consumer. Sport fans are a unique category of consumer because, as previously discussed, sport fans tend to exhibit high levels of identification and involvement with the brand.

Service-based brands are thought to operate along a continuum of consumer involvement and emotional commitment to the brand (Underwood, Bond, and Baer 2001). Sport fans are considered to be among the most highly involved and emotionally attached of any consumer group (Cliffe and Motion 2005). For sport fans, interest and involvement with the sport brand continues even after the service transaction has ended (Funk and James 2001). For highly identified fans, their connection with the team manifests itself through outward actions such as wearing clothing associated with the team or participating in online sport communities. Conversely, less identified sport fans may watch a game and quickly forget about it. This distinction is important, because brands must target marketing efforts to the different levels of involvement among consumers.

The consumption of a service-based brand is a process rather than an outcome (Gronroos 2004). For product-based brands, the transaction between the brand and the consumer is one time and the emphasis is on the consumer taking ownership of the product; however, for service-based brands, the act of consuming the service produced by the brand is an on-going process. The consumption of services, or in the case of sport brands, becomes a series of interactions rather than a one-time transaction. For example, a sport fan who attends a game commits time and money to consume the product (i.e., the game). Due to their high level of involvement with the sport brand, sport fans are more likely to interact and consume the service of the sport brand. As such, consumers of service brands often engage in a long-term relationship with the brand (Gronroos 1994).

Service-based brands rely on an involved consumer base for success. Thus, predicating the need for service-based brands to develop lasting relationships with consumers. This principle holds true for sport brands as well, who depend on highly identified and involved sport fans for financial support and viability. Identified fans are more likely to spend time and money to follow the team including attending games, purchasing team-licensed merchandise, and encourage others to attend games (Meng, Stavros, and Westberg 2015). Similarly, teams with a larger, more involved fan base are attractive to potential sponsors and can demand higher broadcast rights (Heere and James 2007).

CONCLUSION

This chapter provided a foundation for understanding why fan-team relationships are important from both the fan and the team perspective. Sport fans are people who have self-selected and socially identified themselves as sport fans. Through their fandom, sport fans meet their need to feel like they belong with a group. As identification with a team increases, so do activities related to following the team, including seeking out information related to the team, finding outlets to publicly identify with the team, and providing emotional support for the team. In addition, sport fans provide teams with financial support through attending games and purchasing team-licensed products.

The nature of sport as a service rather than a product-based brand makes it an ideal situation for the development of fan-team relationships (representing consumer-brand relationships), as will be discussed in the following chapters. As previously mentioned, sport fans provide sport brands with considerable financial and emotional support, thus it is in the best interest of the team to maintain an engaged and happy fanbase. One way to do that is to develop meaningful relationships with fans using social media.

Chapter 2

Getting Social

In 2015, the NBA's Atlanta Hawks hosted a Swipe Right Night for fans using Tinder, a popular dating app. During a home game, fans were encouraged to use the dating app to connect with other fans at the game. A special suite, complete with roses and breath mints, was set up for those who met their "match" on Tinder and wanted to watch the game together. Couples who wanted to enter the suite showed their phone and match to an to employee and were allowed to enter the suite for the remainder of the game. Though unconventional, this promotion was successful, resulting in national media attention from *USA Today*, *The Today Show*, ESPN, *Sports Illustrated*, and *Bleacher Report*, and reportedly earning the franchise millions in earned media (AgencyCSE 2015). Swipe Right Night caught the attention of the online world, where the promotion results in both the Hawks and Tinder trending on Twitter. Perhaps the most surprising result of this endeavor was that in 2018 Ben McCleskey and Avery Armstrong, a couple who met at the initial Swipe Right Night in 2015, were married in Phillips arena where the Hawks play their home games (Rapaport 2018).

Peter Sorckoff, Atlanta Hawks Chief Creative Officer and SVP of Marketing shared how Swipe Right night came to be (AgencyCSE 2015). Sorckoff explained the team was looking for a way to connect with Millennials when Tinder was suggested. The idea was controversial at first due to the reputation of Tinder as a "hook up" app, but when the team spoke to representatives at Tinder, they reassured them the app was about being "the quickest easiest way for people to meet each other when they are in proximity" (AgencyCSE 2015). It was at that point the Hawks team realized they were on to something. As Sorckoff explained

> [T]he night doesn't have to be about hooking up, the night can be about connecting with likeminded people who you are in proximity with, i.e., another chance for emotional connectedness, another chance for people who otherwise might never intersect each other in their life to come together under the flag or umbrella of your Atlanta Hawks. (AgencyCSE 2015)

In this quote, Sorckoff makes an important point to remember about the fan-team relationship—it's about connecting with others under the banner of sport. And when deep, meaningful connections are made between fans and teams, and fans and fans, then that strengthens the sport brand. This is just one example of how sport brands can utilize the power of social media to connect fans with one another and the organization. It is also a great example of how creativity and innovation can help merge the online and offline experience of sport fans.

Social media and sports have become so interconnected that Sports Illustrated curates a list called the "Social 100" ("Sports Illustrated Social 100"). This list includes the Twitter 100 (the 100 best sport figures to follow on Twitter) and the Top 100 Teams on Twitter, as well as the Ten Best Follows on Facebook, Instagram, and the now defunct Vine. Sport brands have been among the most innovative in terms of integrating social media into its integrated marketing communication efforts, and as a result sport fans have responded by becoming some of the most fervent social media users (Thompson et al. 2014).

Sport brands are smart to embrace social media as a tool to connect with fans as well as to enhance the fan experience online and while watching a game. One could argue that not since the invention of cable television has a technology changed the sport industry quite like social media. As one public relations executive put it, "to communicate effectively, organizations must go to where their stakeholders are" (DiStaso, McCorkindale, and Wright 2011, 326), and for sports brands that place is social media where sport fans are among the most avid group of social media users. Nielsen reports that 60 percent of sports fans check sport-related content on their smartphone or tablet daily (MediaPostNews 2013). A 2016 survey by MediaPost revealed "millennial sport fans are craving digital platforms, sports content and sport social influencers bringing them the content they want to consumer" (Urban 2016). More specifically, this report found 87 percent of eighteen- to twenty-four-year-olds use social media to consume sport related content. Furthermore, nearly 40 percent of sports fans say that using social media to follow their favorite sport team has increased their perceived level of team identification (Moyer, Pokrywczynski, and Griffing 2015). This is important, because as discussed in the previous chapter, identification with the team is an important factor in relationship building.

Prior to social media, fans could only watch a game if they lived near the team to attend games or if the team happened to be playing on television. Fans would have to wait for the evening news to see sport highlights and check box scores in the next morning's paper. But social media has revolutionized this experience. Fans can keep up with games and stats in real time using Twitter, they can interact with other fans using Facebook, and they can get a behind-the-scenes look at the team using Instagram and Snapchat. By connecting with their favorite team via social media, sport fans can gain insider access to the team and have opportunities to interact with their favorite athletes that were once reserved for chance encounters at games. And all of these changes are occurring in real-time, allowing sport fans, a group that was previously anonymous and disjointed, the opportunity to come together and form communities around their favorite teams (Mahan and McDaniel 2006). Relationships thrive off interactions and social media provides another inter-action point that can help strengthen the fan-team relationship.

For sport fans, the use of social media enhances the fan experience like never before (Sanderson and Kassing 2014). Social media allows sport fans to engage with teams on social media and seek information about the team in a more customized environment (Clavio and Walsh 2014; Thompson et al. 2014). DiMoro (2015) notes, "[S]ocial media is a powerful vehicle that drives sports talk today and the way fans interact with teams, players, personalities and fellow fans. It's a powerful source for getting news, engaging in topical discussions and empowering brands." As previously discussed, social media has changed the sport industry and the way fans and teams interact with one another. As such, it is necessary to critically examine the ways in which sport brands and fans use social media and how these interactions can enhance the fan-team relationship.

AN OVERVIEW OF SOCIAL MEDIA

Earlier definitions of social media tended to focus more on the technological distinctions of social media. For example, Kaplan and Haenlein (2010) defined social media as "a group of Internet-based applications that build on the ideological and technological foundations of Web 2.0, and that allow the creation and exchange of User Generated Content" (p. 61). Kohli, Suri, and Kapoor (2015, 37) proffered this definition of social media, "consumer generated media that covers a variety of sources of online information, created by consumers intent on sharing information." According to this definition, the ability of the user to create content is a defining characteristic of social media and further illustrates the nuances of interactivity on social media, which is consistent with the assumption that the high levels of interaction among users distinguishes social media from other types of media (Williams and Chinn 2010). Kietzmann et al. (2011) identified seven features, or building blocks, of social media: (1) identity, (2) conversations, (3) sharing, (4) presence, (5) relationships, (6) reputation, and (7) groups. In other words, social media users can use various social media platforms to present themselves to others, engage in conversations with other users, share content with other users, establish a social presence, engage in relationships, manage their reputation, and join online groups or communities. The term social media is often used as an umbrella term that encapsulates all different types on online activity (Kaplan and Haenlein 2011b) that occurs on social networking sites.

Social networking sites are a more specific form of social media. Boyd and Ellison (2008) were among the first to offer a definition of social networking sites. In their seminal article, they define social networking sites as "web-based services that allow individuals to (1) construct a public or semi-public profile within a bounded system, (2) articulate a list of other users with whom they share a connection, and (3) view and traverse their list of connections and those made by others within the system" (p. 211). They go on to suggest that "what makes social network sites unique is not that they allow individuals to meet strangers, but rather they enable users to articulate and make visible their social networks" (p. 211). One of the earliest social networking sites was SixDegrees.com, which launched in 1997. Between 1997 and 2006, a number of social networking sites were launched including LiveJournal, Friendster, LinkedIn, Bebo, Facebook, YouTube, and MySpace. Friendster, launched in 2002, was among the earliest social networking sites to reach the mainstream, but ultimately failed because of technical issues as a result of the rapid growth (Boyd and Ellison 2008). After Friendster, people flocked to MySpace as the next big thing in social networking sites. MySpace thrived thanks to interest in the site among teenagers and musicians (Boyd and Ellison 2008).

Despite these early successes, it was Facebook that made social media mainstream. Launched in February of 2004 at Harvard University, Facebook was initially a closed social networking site available only at colleges and universities. As the site grew in popularity, it opened the network to allow high school students, corporations, and eventually anyone to create a profile on the site. As of March 2018, there were 1.45 billion daily active Facebook users and 2.20 billion monthly active users ("Company Info" 2018).

After the success of Facebook, other social networking sites emerged offering users niche experiences. For example, Twitter, launched in 2006, was the first microblogging site, allowing users to post messages of 140-characters or less. Four years later, 2010 was a big year for more visually oriented social media platforms when both Pinterest and Instagram were launched. More recently, Snapchat expanded on the visually based social networking phenomenon by making content ephemeral. Snapchat users can share pictures that disappeared after a set amount of time. Statista (2018) reports Facebook, Instagram, and Twitter to be the most popular mobile social networking sites in the United States.

Facebook

Despite the seemingly constant development of new platforms, Facebook remains the most popular with nearly eight-in-ten Americans using Facebook (Greenwood, Perrin, and Duggan 2016). The emergence of Facebook signified a shift toward increased use of social networking sites. For example, Pronschinske, Groza, and Walker (2012) report the number of people using the social networking site outnumbered the people using email to communicate. As previously discussed, Facebook was initially created as an online networking platform for college students but has since expanded its reach to allow commercial organizations to create pages and by 2006, nearly 22,000 organizations created Facebook profiles (Pronschinske, Groza, and Walker 2012).

Researchers have examined the use of Facebook as a branding and relationship-building tool in sports. Wallace, Wilson, and Miloch (2011) examined the Facebook profiles of NCAA teams in the Big 12 athletic conference to determine how teams were using Facebook as part of their brand strategy. Results suggested that the teams used Facebook to promote product-related attributes to further the brand image. Pronschinske, Groza, and Walker (2012) used the relationship marketing framework to analyze how sports teams can use Facebook to attract fans. Results indicated that pages deemed to be authentic had high levels of user engagement and a greater impact on attracting and maintaining a Facebook fan base. Moyer, Pokrywczynski, and Griffing (2015) found that using a team's Facebook page significantly increased levels of identification with the team. The researchers go on to suggest that the resulting increased identification should procure special treatment from the sports brand.

Instagram

Visual-based social media are among the fastest growing social networking sites (McNely 2012), and Instagram is among the largest with more than 800 million active users on the site (Balakrishnan and Boorstin 2017). Founded in 2010 as a free mobile app, Instagram grew rapidly to over 150 million active monthly users who upload 55 million photos per day ("The Complete History of Instagram" 2014). A recent study by the Pew Research Center found Instagram to be the second most popular social networking site, replacing Twitter on the list (Greenwood, Perrin, and Duggan 2016).

Instagram allows users to upload and share images, short videos, and stories with followers. Instagram is unique from other social networking sites in that was developed and primarily functions as a mobile app. In 2011, Instagram was named the iPhone App of the Year ("The Complete History of Instagram" 2014).

Instagram is an emerging powerhouse for brands, where "each Instagram photo has the potential to act as a significant pivot for interaction among audiences of a savvy organization" (McNely 2012, 7). Engagement rates, defined by likes and comments, are generally higher on Instagram than Facebook and Twitter (Salomon 2013). For sports, recent report from AdWeek found that one-in-three Instagram users follow a sports-related account (Heine 2016). Additionally, Instagram has been heralded for its ability to show live action game highlights through its video feature (Sarconi 2017). Sport teams can encourage engagement by incorporating content from fans (Hambrick and Kang 2014).

To date, few published studies have investigated the use of Instagram for sports. Smith and Sanderson (2015) examined the self-presentation strategy of athletes, and Geurin-Eagleman and Burch (2016) also looked at how Olympic athletes used Instagram for self-presentation. Watkins and Lee (2016) examined the effectiveness of Instagram for communicating brand personality and found that Instagram was useful for communicating brand identity; more specifically, teams can communicate brand personality elements using the visual capabilities of Instagram.

Twitter

Twitter is a microblogging site that allows users to "tweet" news and information to their followers using 140-characters or less (Kaplan and Haenlein 2011a). The purpose of Twitter is to provide users with an outlet for posting short messages about what they are doing, share observations, and provide information to followers. Within the Twitter platform, users act as both the audience and the producer of content (Frederick et al. 2012). One of the defining features of Twitter is that users are more likely to interact with others who are not part of their immediate social network. Another defining feature of Twitter is the ease with which one could engage in direct two-way communication with other users, including brands (Kwon and Sung 2011). However, much of the research focusing on brand interactions on Twitter indicates that this capability is largely underutilized (Levenshus 2010).

Twitter is arguably better suited for interactions between users and brand (Smith 2010) and has been especially useful for sports brands that want to leverage fans' online involvement. Twitter aids in building consumer-brand relationships by enabling brands to speak directly to consumers without going through the filter of traditional media and allowing consumers to communicate with one another (Mangold and Faulds 2009). By using the dialogic capabilities of the medium, sports organizations are able to connect with fans on a more intimate, interpersonal level (Clavio and Kian 2010).

Twitter use is prevalent in sports (Frederick et al. 2012), with anyone from athletes to coaches to sports journalists using the site as a platform to provide fans with immediate access to information (Browning and Sanderson 2012; Pegoraro 2010). Sport brands use Twitter to connect with fans, provide information, sell tickets, promote the team, and increase overall brand awareness (Hambrick et al. 2010). Over the last decade, researchers have examined how Twitter has been integrated in sport culture. For example, some studies have looked at how athletes use Twitter to interact with fans (Browning and Sanderson 2012; Frederick et al. 2012; Pegoraro 2010) and how fans use social media (Kassing and Sanderson 2010; Smith and Smith 2012). Still other researchers have looked at Twitter use from the team perspective, focusing on how sport brands use Twitter to engage in relationship-building activities with fans (Abeza, O'Reilly, and Reid 2013; Clavio and Kian 2010; Frederick, Hambrick, and Clavio 2014; Watkins 2017).

From the sport fan perspective, using Twitter allows fans unprecedented access to their favorite teams and athletes. These types of interactions can allow fans to "develop a greater appreciation for the talent, dedication to their sport, and the day-to-day lives of those athletes" (Pegoraro 2010, 504). Sports fans are avid Twitter users (Frederick et al. 2012). Twitter has been described as "the virtual sports bar that fans flock to before, during, and after the game" (DiMoro 2015). For example, sport fans are 67 percent more likely to use Twitter as a second-screen to enhance the game watching experience (DiMoro 2015). Twitter is a useful platform for sports fans in that it allows them to "create personalized spaces where they can express support for their favorites and discuss sports" (Hambrick et al. 2010, 455).

As outlined above, the prevalent use of Twitter in sports and the impact the platform has had on the sport industry makes it an ideal context for studying how social media can be used to enhance the fan-team relationship. Twitter embodies the potential of social media for two-way communication between brands and consumers and provides an outlet for fans to interact with one another. The research presented in later chapters examines to what extent Twitter is useful as a fan-team relationship-building tool, the content strategies sport teams use on Twitter to connect with fans, and subsequently, an evaluation of the effectiveness of these strategies. There are a number of social media platforms available for this kind of research, and future research should take on that challenge, but focusing energy and resources into an in-depth examination of Twitter will help provide a foundation to support future research endeavors.

SOCIAL MEDIA FOR STRATEGIC COMMUNICATION

Social media and social networking sites have had a profound effect on how brands approach interactions with consumers. The interactive nature of social media has resulted in an empowered consumer group who now expects brands to be more transparent and responsive (Kerpen 2015). This has led brands to reconsider not only marketing efforts but the brand's overall philosophy toward communicating and engaging with audiences. Termed *social organizations*, Kim (2016) refers to these organizations as "brands that recognize social interaction as a *core approach* to business rather than social media as a *tool* to accomplish business, and thus experience the power of authentic relationships with key stakeholders" (p. 2; emphasis added). As such, brands are devoting more resources toward social media strategy. Effing and Spil (2010) define social media strategy as "a goal-directed planning process for creating user generated content, driven by a group of Internet applications, to create a unique and valuable competitive position" (p. 2). In other words, to effectively use social media, brands must develop a strategic, goal-oriented plan for how to engage and interact with audiences. Effective social media use has the potential to engage important stakeholder groups in meaningful conversation (Kim 2016). Based on a systematic literature review of research focusing on strategic social media Effing and Spil (2016) found target audience, channel choice, goals, resources, policies, monitoring, and content activities to be key elements of social media strategy.

The shift to a more strategic approach to social media requires brands to understand the purpose and nature of social media—relationships. Brands that do not understand the nature of social media will not succeed on social media (Luttrell 2014). Effective strategic social media use requires going beyond traditional advertising, marketing, and public relations principles of one-way broadcasting of information toward a focus on interaction and relationship building with audiences. Luttrell (2014) breaks down the individual meanings of the words *social* and *media* to capture the relational component of social media:

> [S]ocial is the need that we, as human beings, have to connect with others through companionship via relationships with others in society, either individually or in groups. . . . The word *media* relates to the channels through which we make connections with others (p. 22)

According to Luttrell's (2014) argument, by breaking down the term social media into the essence of each word's individual meaning, we arrive at the true purpose of social media—relationship building through online channels. Kim (2016) reiterates this point through proposing the social principle, which states "the fluid nature of social media is designed for and sustained in *relationship* through two-way communication around topics of mutual interest that is user-initiated, -created, and -driven" (p. 4, emphasis added). If a brand, including sport brands, wants to be successful using social media it must realize that relationships not selling is the foundation of social media use. The approach and commitment to relationship building must go beyond posting on social networking sites but must also represent the brand's values.

CONNECTING ON SOCIAL MEDIA

Social media has given rise to a more active and empowered consumer across all sectors, including sports. Social media users not only control what information they take in, but also what they choose to share with others in their online social network (Kohli, Suri, and Kapoor 2015). As such, "consumers have become pivotal authors of brand stories" (Gensler et al. 2013, 244). Social media allows fans to follow along with games when they are not able to watch, interact with other fans, participate in fantasy sports leagues, and comment on relevant sports stories. Social media allows sport fans to have a voice where they can praise, complain, or seek customer services directly from the brand (Williams and Chinn 2010). Using social media, sports fans can extend their fanship networks by posting original content to sports-related social networking sites, message boards, blogs, and mobile apps (Gantz and Lewis 2014). This helps fans connect not only with the team but with other fans. Content created by other users is considerably more impactful than content created by the organization itself (Gensler et al. 2013). As such, for the sport fan using social media to follow their favorite team can enhance the overall experience of being a fan, which can result in increased identification with the team (Arvidsson 2006; Browning and Sanderson 2012; Hambrick et al. 2010; Phua 2010).

One of the defining characteristics that distinguishes sport fans from consumers of other service-based brands is the sport fan's desire to be associated with the sport brand (Shani 1997). Team involvement manifests through consuming games (in person and on television), purchasing team licensed memorabilia, and publicly expressing fandom with the team. Involvement with a sports brand has been cited as a factor that increases identification with a sports team (Sutton et al. 1997). Using social media, sport fans have virtually unlimited opportunities to publicly express their fandom and connect with their favorite teams and athletes (Pegoraro 2010) as well as an avenue for fans to connect with one another. Online access to sports teams through websites, social media, and mobile apps is beneficial for sports fans who are willing to login daily to catch up on the news about their favorite team (Seo and Green 2008).

Sport brands benefit from a more active and involved consumer base. High levels of consumer engagement actually help to strengthen a brand (Enginkaya and Yilmaz 2014). Brands that do well in the social media environment embrace the empowered consumer, but also provide content and services that meet their needs. For most people, the decision to identify with an organization is influenced by brand communication, experience, and reference groups (Boyle and Magnusson 2007). When fans participate in sports-related social media, they report higher levels of fan identification and collective self-esteem (Phua 2010).

Sport brands can take a more active role in connecting with fans. Gladden, Irwin, and Sutton (2001) list four ways that sport teams can enhance the fan-team relationship: (1) seek ways to understand the consumer, (2) create opportunities for interaction between the brand and the consumer, (3) reward customer loyalty, and (4) integrate marketing associations to maintain a consistent message across platforms. Using social media, sport brands can achieve these things through social listening, creating compelling content that encourages interactivity and engagement, hosting online contests, and integrating online and offline marketing efforts.

From the sports-brand perspective, social media allows the brand to interact and engage with fans in an authentic and engaging manner (Filo, Lock, and Karg 2015). Sport brands can benefit from online fan engagement in the following ways: (1) better knowledge of sport participants and fans, (2) advanced customer-organization interaction, (3) effective customer engagement, (4) efficient use of resources (i.e., time and money), and (5) quicker evaluation of the customer-organization relationship status (Abeza, O'Reilly, and Reid 2013). To engage in relationship building with sport fans, it is important for sport brands to create positive associations with sport fans and provide opportunities for collaboration that enhances the importance of the relationship (Abeza and O'Reilly 2014; Meng, Stavros, and Westberg 2015; Waters and Walden 2015).

CONCLUSION

This chapter examined social media and how the tools of social media can be used to enhance the fan-team relationship. As previously discussed, social media is about building relationships—whether it is a relationship with long lost friends from high school or a favorite brand. The networks built into social media platforms provide a connection that transcends geographical boundaries in ways not possible before. For brands that depend on strong, lasting relationships with consumers, such as sport brands, social media provides an interesting and innovative set of tools to connect and interact with audiences.

In order for sport brands to be successful on social media they must understand the audience and what the audiences needs and wants from the brand on social media. As such, the goal of this book is to look at both sides of using social media to build, enhance, and maintain the fan-team relationship. The previous chapters reviewed the key players (sport brands and fans), why relationships are important, how both parties benefit from strong fan-team relationships, and why social media is an important tool in the relationship-building process. The missing piece, not yet discussed, is what happens when the two groups come together online. Teams can create content, fans can go online and use the platform, but there is limited research that looks at what happens when these two sides come together. Using the concept of engagement (explained in depth in the next chapter), empirical research will be presented that looks at how engagement between fans and sport teams can result in stronger fan-team relationships.

Chapter 3

Online Fan Engagement and Fan-Team Relationships

The two-way communication capabilities of social media have given rise to a new kind of consumer. In the past, people tended to passively consume media content, but social media has created "a seismic shift in consumers' behavior" (Kohli, Suri, and Kapoor 2015, 37), a consumer who is empowered and more involved with brand (Bitter, Grabner-Krauter, and Breitenecker 2014). Consumers are increasingly using the power of social media to demand that brands are transparent and held accountable for their actions. As such, the advent of social media has led to an increase in consumer-brand involvement. Consumer-brand involvement is the "level of interest in, and personal relevance of a brand" (Hollebeek, Glynn, and Brodie 2014, 149). In other words, involvement represents what can be considered the first level of relationship building, where the consumer has found the brand to be personally relevant. The more relevant the brand is for the consumer, then the more likely the consumer is to seek out other ways to connect with the brand. This is especially relevant in the sport context where fans tend to be more involved with the sport brand in general as a result of increased identification with the brand (Underwood, Bond, and Baer 2001).

Over time, involvement with the brand can lead to increased levels of engagement, which is hypothesized to lead to the development of mutually beneficial fan-team relationships. However, to date, much of the research in this area is largely conceptual with few studies available to provide empirical support for this relationship. The research presented in this chapter aims to be among the first to provide such support and advance understanding of how online engagement through Twitter can be used to facilitate the relationship-building process. Using an online survey of self-identified sport fans who use Twitter, this study uses statistical analysis to explicate to what extent online Twitter engagement influences loyalty, self-brand connection, and the overall perception of the fan-team relationship. First, however, it is beneficial to review the concept of consumer-brand relationships, which provides the theoretical foundation for understanding fan-team relationships as well as the various approaches to measuring online engagement.

CONSUMER-BRAND RELATIONSHIPS

Whether they realize it or not, brands are important part of the everyday lives of consumers and are often important in the development of individual identity (Tuškej, Golob, and Podnar 2013) and consumers who have a strong psychological identification with a brand are most desirable for brands (Kunkel, Doyle, and Funk 2014). Consumer-brand relationships have received a considerable amount of attention in marketing literature. Brand relationships represent a long and established bond between the consumer and brand (Morgan-Thomas and Veloutsou 2013), and are defined as "the psychological bonds formed between the consumer and the brand" (Tsai 2011, 1194). The fundamental principle guiding research of consumer-brand relationships is that people, in many ways, interact with brands following the conventions of interpersonal relationships with people (Aggarwal 2004; Fournier 1998; Fournier and Alvarez 2012). In other words, it is widely accepted among scholars and practitioners that people and brands can and do enter into relationships with one another. The foundation of a consumer-brand relationship is the consumer's understanding what the brand is and the value they attribute to that brand. In these relationships, brands are treated as people (Fournier and Alvarez, 2012) and follow the socially accepted norms of interpersonal communication (Kim, Park, and Kim 2014). According to Aggarwal (2004) when brands act in ways that is consistent with the norms of the culture, then those rules govern the interaction of brands.

Brand relationships involve (1) a reciprocal exchange between the consumer and the brand, (2) where each party finds meaning and value in the relationship, (3) there are many different types of consumer-brand relationships, and (4) these relationships can evolve over time (Fournier 1998). In a sport context, sport fans engage in relationships with sport teams much in the same way consumers enter into relationships with other brands. For example, the reciprocal exchange between sport brand and fan revolves around attending and watching games and purchasing team-licensed merchandise.

As previously discussed, service-based brands, like sport brands, operate in a market that is often unpredictable and requires sustained commitment from sport fans over long periods of time. It is the fan-team relationship that sustains teams during times of uncertainty and losing seasons. Think about this in the context of the long-suffering sport teams who go decades without winning a championship. A brand with a strong relationship with fans can survive what are sometimes extended periods of losing. To that end, strong consumer-brand relationships (or fan-team relationships in this case) should be based on mutually beneficial exchanges rather than transactions (Tsai 2011). In other words, the value should come not only from the service but the experience of consuming the service. This leads to the assumption that relationships are co-created, with each party expressing interest in entering and maintaining the relationship. The word maintaining is key here as it indicates effort must be made by both parties to sustain the relationship.

The brand's role in the relationship is to maximize performance in order to satisfy the utilitarian and affective needs of the consumer. The service brand establishes the relationship with the consumer by providing the intended service in a way that is valuable and meaningful for the consumer. Doing so establishes trust and commitment with the consumer and over time, through frequent interactions, the two parties develop a common understanding (Abeza and O'Reilly 2014). In addition to providing core services, brands should seek to understand, communicate, and maintain ongoing interactions with consumers (Simmons 2007). In a sport context, this requires the sport brand to put the best possible product on the field or court, create unique fan experiences, and engage in regular interactions with fans.

In a consumer-brand context, the brand must communicate the benefits of choosing the service or product over the competitor, but the decision to engage with the brand comes from the consumer. According to relationship theory, relationships are an ongoing process between two parties that result in a meaningful experience, and consumers are active and selective about the brands in which they choose to identify with (Dwyer, Greenhalgh, and LeCrom 2015). Active involvement on the part of the consumer is what precipitates the consumers' desire to associate with and commit to the brand, thus enabling the formation of a consumer-brand relationship (Tuškej, Golob, and Podnar 2013).

Sport fans value experiences with their favorite sport team that go beyond watching a game (Stavros et al. 2014), which provides support for the need to create unique and personalized online experiences between the sport brand and fans. The interactive nature of social media creates the possibility that fans can communicate directly with their favorite team or athletes as well as other fans (Abeza, O'Reilly, and Reid 2013; Hambrick et al. 2010). The experience that sport fans have with their favorite team over a sustained amount of time is an indicator of the likelihood for continued involvement and engagement with the team (Van Doorn et al. 2010). As such, it is proposed here that engagement, specifically online engagement, with a sport brand will have positive influence on the development of fan-team relationships.

DEVELOPING FAN-TEAM RELATIONSHIPS

Before assessing the influence of engagement on the fan-team relationship, it is necessary to review the process that leads to fan-team relationships. It is argued here that the starting point for the fan-team relationship is the fan, who according to social identity theory self-selects and chooses to identify with a particular sport team. Social identity theory positions the individual as an active participant in choosing which groups to identify with. Fan identification, then, is the identification one has with a sport brand and as identification with the brand increases it becomes internalized and an important self-identifying feature for sport fans.

As fan identification becomes a salient self-identifying feature, fans seek out ways to enhance their connection with the team, including the use of social media sites like Twitter. In a study examining brand outcomes of social media use, Watkins (2014b) found fan identification to have a significant, positive influence on using Twitter and team-based mobile apps to follow their favorite sport team. The Watkins (2014b) study did not provide insights into how activity on those social media platforms (i.e., engagement) translated into specific brand-related outcomes, but what this study does is provide support for the fan identification as the starting point for engaging with the sport brand and subsequently the development of a fan-team relationship. The research presented within this chapter will investigate to what extent online engagement dimensions influence outcomes related to the fan-team relationship. Specifically, this research looks at how online engagement influences the self-brand connection and loyalty in addition the fan-team relationship.

Self-Brand Connection

Central to the development of a strong consumer-brand relationship is a "self-brand connection" that resonates on a personal level with the consumer (Fournier and Yao 1997, 461). Consumer brand identification is "the perception of sameness between the brand (signifying an object with symbolic meanings) and the consumer" (Tuškej, Golob, and Podnar 2013, 53). Consumers choose to identify with brands that meet one or more of their self-definitional needs (Bhattacharya and Sen 2003). Brands that are able to make an emotional connection with consumers also tend to reflect the consumer's values (Berry 2000). Likewise, consumers who choose to identify with a brand likely do so based on the shared values they hold with the brand (Underwood, Bond, and Baer 2001).

For a relationship to be successful, both parties should share common values. Values are "enduring consumer beliefs about specific modes of conduct or end states" (Bee and Kahie 2006, 104). Brand values are often exhibited through the intangible characteristics of the brand (Tuškeg, Golob, and Podnar 2013). It is the job of the brand to understand and communicate the consumer's values in a way that the consumer will identify with the brand (Berry 2000). When a consumer finds that they share similar values with a brand, then they will be more likely to identify with the brand on a personal or social level. This identification, in turn, leads to a commitment to the brand and ultimately the development of a consumer-brand relationship (Tuškeg, Goloab, and Podnar 2013).

Relationships that center on a shared set of values between the consumer and the brand are more likely to be sustained over the long term and withstand external threats to the relationship (Bee and Kahie 2006). Value congruency, or the alignment of the individual's values with the brand, is especially important for the fan-team relationship (Tuškej, Golob, and Podnar 2013). Value alignment with sport brands, players, and coaches enhances the intensity of fan behavior (Bee and Kahie 2006). For many sport consumers, their fandom is often a self-defining characteristic (Donavan, Carlson, and Zimmerman 2005), and as such the team needs to not only exhibit positive traits but should also align with the fan's core values. For example, if a sport fans values giving back to the community, then sport brands that exhibit a strong sense of corporate social responsibility and giving back to the local community becomes one of the many factors that influence the consumer decision to enter into a consumer-brand relationship with a sport brand.

Loyalty

Identification with a brand can lead to increased brand commitment and loyalty on the part of the consumer (Tuškej, Golob, and Podnar 2013). Loyalty is "steadfast allegiance to a person or cause" (Funk and James 2006, 190) and is considered to be the result of a relationship between attitude and likelihood to repurchase a product (Karjaluoto, Munnukka, and Salmi 2016). In a brand context, loyalty to a brand results in repeat buying behavior that results from favorable beliefs and attitudes toward the brand (Keller 1993). In a sport context, sport team loyalty is "a psychological attachment to a team resulting in positive behaviors and attitudes toward that team" (Dwyer, Greenhalgh, and LeCrom 2015, 644). When considering loyalty from both the brand and sport perspective, a loyal fanbase is important because the deep attachments fans have to the team can result in a long-lasting relationship and an increased likelihood to engage in repeat purchase behavior.

Sport team loyalty reflects deeply held attitudes and beliefs about the team, which increases the connection between the fan and the team that is persistent and resistant to change (Funk and James 2001). Furthermore, loyalty toward a sport team is developed through regular interactions with the team (Gladden, Irwin, and Sutton 2001). Team loyalty is used interchangeably with commitment to a team, but when considering implications for a fan-team relationship, this is not always the case. Loyalty to a team represents a deeper level of involvement with the team. Heere and Dickeson (2008, 227) explain, "[C]ommitment is internal to the individual, whereas loyalty is longitudinal in nature and should be regarded as the result of interaction between negative external changes in the environment and the individual's internal level of commitment." In other words, sport fans exhibit loyalty to the team by maintaining social identification with the team over an extended period of time. The deep connection and loyalty sport fans have for their favorite team explains how fans stick with their favorite team despite consistent losing seasons.

Beyond support for the team, sport fans who express loyalty to a team develop a positive attitude toward the team and engage in repeat purchase behavior in the same way a loyal retail chain customer would. We can look at a common retail example to clarify these concepts; there are people who are loyal to Starbucks and those who are loyal to Dunkin' Donuts. Depending on which brand they are loyal to some fans will argue that one brand of coffee is superior to the other (i.e., attitude formation) and will only visit their favorite store for their morning coffee (i.e., behavioral consistency) even when presented with other options. Sport team loyalty operates much in the same manner. Once a fan has identified with a team and claimed it as their own, their attitude will shift to reflect their positive feelings for the team (i.e., arguing for the team's potential even in the midst of a losing season) and behavioral consistency through the purchase of tickets and team-licensed merchandise.

The purpose of this chapter is to examine the influence of online engagement on the self-brand connection, loyalty, and the fan-team relationship. The previous sections provided the foundation for understanding the dependent variables, the following section will review the relevant research on the online engagement to provide an overview of the independent variables in this study.

ONLINE ENGAGEMENT FOR RELATIONSHIP BUILDING

To this point is has been established that the success of a sport brand depends on the maintenance of mutually beneficial relationships between the sport brand and fans. This book positions social media as an important and effective tool to connect sport fans and teams, which can ultimately have a positive influence on fan-team relationships. Active online engagement from fans constitutes an online relationship with the team where fan activity represents buy-in from fans (Gummerus et al. 2012). The central thesis of the research presented in this chapter is that online engagement with a team using Twitter can have a positive influence on the fan-team relationship. Teams should develop a social media strategy that utilizes the structural features of social media in a way that meets the needs of fans and encourages continued online engagement with the team. The back and forth process of online engagement is what aids in the development and enhancement of the fan-team relationship. Therefore, it is important to fully understand the concept of engagement and how it is a necessary component of relationship building. The influx of social media platforms into strategic brand communication has opened the door to scholarly inquiry into the concept of engagement. However, to date, much of this work has been conceptual and focuses primarily on scale development. The research reported in this chapter is an attempt to bring together the various conceptualizations of online engagement and to test their application in the sport context in order to provide empirical support for the use of Twitter as a relationship-building tool.

DEFINING ENGAGEMENT

The interactive nature of social media has given way to increased attention and interest among scholars about the nature of engagement between brands and consumers. In particular, there has been an uptick in scholarly activity examining the topic from a variety of disciplinary and theoretical perspectives. As a result, numerous definitions for engagement have been suggested. For example, Vivek, Beatty, and Morgan's (2012) definition of customer engagement is frequently cited in the literature. They define engagement as "the intensity of an individual's participation in and connection with an organization's offerings and/or organizational activities, which either the customer or the organization initiate" (p. 127). Brodie et al. (2011) present a more comprehensive definition of engagement:

> Customer engagement (CE) is a psychological state that occurs by virtue of interactive, co-creative customer experiences with a focal agent/object (e.g., a brand) in focal service relationships. It occurs under a specific set of context-dependent conditions generating differing CE levels; and exists as a dynamic, iterative process within service relationships that co-create value. (9)

After reviewing the existing literature on consumer engagement, Islam and Rahman (2016) offer this definition of engagement:

> [T]the readiness of a customer to actively participate and interact with the focal object (e.g., brand, organization, community, website, organizational activity), which varies in direction (positive or negative) and magnitude (high or low) depending on the nature of a customer's interaction with various touch points (physical or virtual. (2019)

In other words, engagement reflects a deeper commitment and motivation on the part of the consumer where the consumer is active in pursuing a relationship with the brand. As such, engagement represents a more enhanced relationship with a brand that results in increased value for the consumer and, subsequently, benefits the brand (Brodie et al. 2011).

MEASURING ONLINE ENGAGEMENT

In the context of social media, engagement is often operationalized and evaluated through the number of likes and comments on an organization's social media post. However, as indicated by the previous discussion, engagement is defined as a multidimensional construct, which includes cognitive, emotional, and behavioral dimensions (Brodie et al. 2011; Hollebeek, Glynn, and Brodie 2014). This is reflected in literature related to the development of scales to measure online engagement. Despite the emphasis on multiple dimensions accounting for online engagement, the scales presented in recent years take two different approaches. One scale, developed by Schivinski, Christodoulides, and Dabrowski (2016) focuses on the behavioral components of online engagement while the second approach, proposed by Hollebeek et al. (2014), measures engagement based on cognitive/affective dimensions. Given the relative newness of this research in a social media context, it is worthwhile to investigate both approaches to engagement to provide a more holistic approach to understanding online engagement.

Behavioral Approaches to Measuring Engagement

Generally speaking consumer-brand engagement behaviors are defined as "a customer's behavioral manifestations that have a brand or firm focus beyond purchase, resulting from motivational drivers" (Van Doorn et al. 2010, 253). This definition includes the online context and suggests that social media can be used to provide word-of-mouth recommendations, write reviews, and blog about the brand. What is important to note with this definition is that the emphasis is on the active role of the consumer. Engagement signifies an active consumer, who participates in sharing values and content with the brand (Hollebeek, Glynn, and Brodie 2014; Islam and Rahman 2016). Furthermore, it is important to understand consumer behaviors with the brand; these behaviors are often an indication of relationship strength.

Schivinski, Christodoulides, and Dabrowski (2016) presented a scale to measure online engagement from a behavioral perspective. The work of Schivinski, Christodoulides, and Dabrowski (2016) is an extension of the Muntinga, Moorman, and Smit's (2011) "Consumer's Online Brand-Related Online Activities" framework by measuring online brand engagement on three dimensions: (1) consuming content, (2) contributing content, and (3) creating content. To support this approach to measuring engagement, the authors proffered the following definition of engagement: "A set of brand-related online activities on the part of the consumer that vary in the degree to which the consumer interacts with social media and engages in the consumption, contribution and creation of media content" (p. 67). According to this definition, while online engagement may be initiated by the brand through the creation of social media content, it is the consumer's choice and responsibility to engage with the brand. Subsequently, this definition proposes three levels of engagement—consuming the content, contributing to the content, or creating new content where the creation of brand-related content represents the highest level of brand engagement. Table 3.1 summarizes the dimensions of engagement outlined in this approach.

Cognitive/Affective Approach to Measuring Engagement

The cognitive and emotional dimensions of consumer-brand engagement reflect the consumer's feelings related to the brand. Scholars argue that because consumer engagement with a brand represents a "stronger state of connectedness" than merely liking social media content (Van Doorn et al. 2010, 254), then methods for evaluating engagement should go beyond behaviors and account for cognitive and affective components of engagement. The idea underpinning this approach to engagement suggests that by creating content that is creative and relevant to consumers, brands can encourage consumers to be more proactive in how they think about the brand to the point where they actively seek out interactions with the brand (Malthouse et al. 2016, 427).

The cognitive/affective approach to measure engagement comes from the work of Hollebeek, Glynn, and Brodie (2014) who developed a scale that measures consumer-brand engagement in online settings. The Hollebeek, Glynn, and Brodie (2014) scale also measures engagement on three dimensions (cognitive engagement, affective engagement, and activation engagement), but unlike the Schivinski, Christodoulides, and Dabrowski (2016) scale, these dimensions represent a deeper, more intimate connection with the brand. Hollebeek, Glynn, and Brodie (2014) define consumer-brand engagement as "a consumer's positively valanced cognitive, emotional and behavioral brand-related activity during, or related to specific consumer/brand interactions" (p. 154). In other words, unlike Schivinski, Christodoulides, and Dabrowski (2016), who focus on the behavioral aspects of engagement only, this approach represents a more holistic view of engagement by capturing cognitive and affective dimensions of engagement. Table 3.1 summarizes the dimensions of engagement represented in these two approaches. Survey questions and item analysis from each of these engagement scales can be found in appendix A.

ASSESSING ONLINE ENGAGEMENT
AND TEAM RELATED OUTCOMES

To this point, this chapter has provided a considerable amount of background information. In summary, the goal of the research presented in this chapter is to provide insights into whether or not online engagement is a significant predictor of the fan-team relationship and to what extent the different approaches to measuring engagement influence the fan-team relationship. Additionally, two other indicators of fan-team relationship, the self-brand connection and loyalty, are also used to help elucidate how engagement can be beneficial for the fan-team relationship. Figure 3.1 illustrates the proposed relationships tested in this research.

Self-identified sport fans were recruited using Amazon Mechanical Turk (MTurk) to participate in an online survey. In order to participate in the study, workers had to (1) identify themselves as a sports fan and (2) use Twitter to follow sports. A total of 456 survey responses were submitted, but only 387 were complete and usable in the analysis. Of the respondents, 75.7% identified as male ($n = 293$) and 24.3% ($n = 94$) identified as female. The average age of respondents was 31.57 ($SD = 9.331$) and the average time they have been a sport fan was 13.61 years ($SD = 11.772$).

Respondents were asked to what extent they considered themselves to be identified as sport fans, and on a 5-point scale, the average score was 4.14 ($SD = 1.033$). This indicates that respondents were strongly self-identified sport fans. The majority of respondents identified as football fans ($n = 161$, 41.6%) followed by basketball ($n = 63$, 16.3%), baseball ($n = 38$, 9.8%), soccer ($n = 35$, 9.0%), and hockey ($n = 24$, 6.2%). When asked how frequently they used Twitter to follow sports, 70.1% of respondents ($n = 271$)

Table 3.1. Approaches to Engagement

Behavioral Dimensions of Engagement (Schiviniski et al. 2016)		
Dimension	*Definition*	*Twitter Example*
Consumption	minimum level of engagement; refers to consumers who passively consumer brand-related media without participating (p. 67)	reading Tweets produced by the team or tweets about the team produced by other Twitter users
Contribution	peer-to-peer and peer-to-content interactions about brands; reflects consumers' contribution to brand-related content through participation in media previously created by either a company of another individual (pg. 67)	the act of liking or retweeting posts created by the team or other Twitter users
Creation	consumers' creation and online publication of brand-related content (p. 67)	replying to a tweet or writing an original tweet about the team

Cognitive/Affective Dimensions of Engagement (Hollebeek et al. 2014)		
Dimension	*Definition*	*Twitter Examples*
Cognitive Processing	a consumer's level of brand-related thought processing and elaboration in a particular consumer/ brand interaction (p. 154)	fans who read tweets related to their favorite team will spend time thinking about the team and the content
Affective	a consumer's degree of positive brand-related affect in a particular consumer/brand interaction (p. 154)	fans correlate positive feelings toward the team with interactions on Twitter
Activation	a consumer's level of energy, effort, and time spent on a brand in a particular consumer/ brand interaction (p. 154)	the amount of time and resources a fan is willing to invest in following their favorite team on Twitter

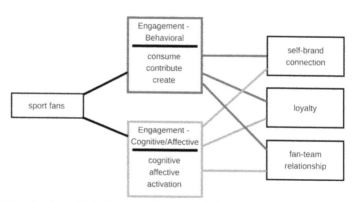

Figure 3.1:   Illustrated Relationships. Courtesy of the author

indicated using the platform at least half the time. Thus, an appropriate sample was collected for this analysis.

After completing the screening questions, respondents were directed to identify their most favorite sport team and answer questions measuring the following variables as it relates to that team: (1) sport spectator identification, (2) fan-team relationship, (3) self-brand connection, (4) loyalty, (5) engagement on Twitter (behavioral), and (6) engagement on Twitter (cognitive/affective). Survey measures and item analysis can be found in appendix A.

SURVEY RESULTS

The first goal of this analysis was to find empirical support for online engagement as a predictor of the three dependent variables—self-brand connection, loyalty, and fan-team relationship. Results of two multiple regression analysis revealed that engagement, both behavioral and cognitive/affective, were found to be significant predictors of each dependent variable. In other words, yes, online engagement can and does influence the self-brand connection between a sport fan and their favorite team, the feelings of loyalty between the fan and the team, and the overall fan-team relationship.

The adjusted R^2 statistics provides an indication of the overall model fit and gives an indication of how well the different approaches to engagement influence the outcome variables. As demonstrated in table 3.2, behavioral dimensions of engagement had the most influence for loyalty whereas cognitive/affective were more influential for self-brand connection and fan-team relationship. This indicates that the deeper, more emotional and thought-provoking dimensions of engagement have a stronger potential to influence self-brand connection and fan-team relationship than loyalty. This makes

Table 3.2. Adjusted R² Comparison

	Behavioral Dimensions of Engagement	Cognitive/Affective Dimensions of Engagement
Loyalty	39.1%	34.0%
Self-Brand Connection	25.9%	35.0%
Fan-Team Relationship	21.5%	37.6%

sense given that self-brand connection and fan-team relationships are largely dependent on self-reflection and identification on the part of the consumer. Loyalty is more influenced by behavioral dimensions of engagement, which given the nature of loyalty as an outward expression of fandom, also provides credence to this finding. Behavioral dimensions of engagement are more visible, tangible expressions of fandom and thus provide a way for a sport fan to demonstrate loyalty.

In sum, the findings of this analysis point to online engagement using Twitter, both from a behavioral and cognitive/affective perspective, to have a positive influence on self-brand connection, loyalty, and fan-team relationship. The cognitive/affective dimensions were more influential when it comes to enhancing the self-brand connection and fan-team relationship; whereas loyalty is influenced most by the behavioral dimensions of engagement. The complete statistical analysis for research reported in this chapter can be found in appendix B and appendix C.

The next goal is to determine to what extent do the various dimensions of engagement influence these outcomes. Recall that there are two approaches to measuring engagement—behavioral and cognitive/affective. Both approaches are statistically significant influences on fan-team relationship, self-brand connection, and loyalty, but a closer look at the analysis will provide insight into how online engagement using Twitter can be an effective relationship-building tool.

Evaluating Behavioral Dimensions of Engagement

As previously discussed, the overall model provides support for behavioral dimensions of engagement (create, contribute, and consume) to have a significant influence on self-brand connection, loyalty, and fan-team relationships. The analysis revealed that among the five types of behavioral engagement (read tweets, like tweets, retweet, reply to tweets, and write tweets) only *read*, *like*, and *write tweets* were found to have an individual significant influence. More specifically, reading tweets and writing tweets (consume and create dimension, respectively) were found to have a statistically significant influence on loyalty. This means that by engaging with the team by reading and writing tweets, fans can enhance their feelings of loyalty to the team. For the self-brand connection, reading and liking tweets were found to have a significant individual influence and for fan-team relationships, only reading tweets had a significant influence.

Now I want to take care to not overstate these findings. As demonstrated in table B.1 (see appendix B), the beta values indicate a low level of influence with values ranging from .185 to .354. In other words, while the influence of these behaviors is statistically significant, there are likely other factors that contribute to the perception of the fan-team relationship. This is not a surprising finding, as the main argument of this book is not that Twitter is the solution to developing strong fan-team relationships, but rather this book is an effort to explain how Twitter can be a tool for facilitating fan-team relationships.

The three dimensions of behavioral engagement identified by Schivinski, Christodoulides, and Dabrowski (2016) represent a continuum of engagement (see figure 3.3). Consuming content represents the lowest form of engagement that requires the least amount of effort on the part of the consumer. The survey operationalized this dimension as reading tweets about one's favorite team. Contributing content represents a more moderate form of engagement, and as indicated in the definition, it represents engagement with preexisting content. In the Twitter context, this means the act of "liking" or "retweeting" content created by another user. Finally, creating content represents the highest-level engagement where a user expends time and resources to create

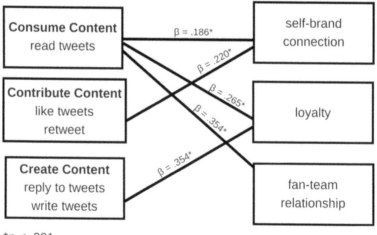

*p < .001

Figure 3.2: Behavioral Dimensions of Engagement. Courtesy of the author

brand-related content. Creating content was operationalized through replying to tweets and writing original tweets.

In the context of the research findings presented in this chapter, among the behavioral dimensions, consuming was the most consistent in terms of predicting fan-team relationships, loyalty, and self-brand connection. In particular, the individual analysis revealed that reading tweets had the strongest impact on the fan-team relationship variable. One possible explanation for this is that through reading tweets produced by the team, fans are able to connect with the team. Most people use Twitter to seek out information; perhaps by meeting the informational needs of fans, sport brands are making a positive contribution to the fan-team relationship.

Results also provide support for creating content, particularly writing original brand-related tweets, as a significant influence on loyalty. Consumers create brand-related, user-generated content to publicly express aspects of their identification with the brand and to interact with other brand enthusiasts (Malthouse et al. 2016). Creating online brand-related content empowers consumers to be more engaged with the brand, where "consumers no longer are satisfied with experiences fabricated by companies; instead, they want to shape experiences themselves through co-created content" (Christodoulides, Jevons, and Bonhomme 2012, 4–5).

In terms of benefits for the brand, consumers can provide feedback to brands through social media posts and participation in online brand communities. This feedback is important for brands as they often provide new ideas for how to improve the product (Van Doorn et al. 2010). For the sport context, this information can help improve fan experience when attending games or provide insight into information and content that fans find to be most useful. Additionally, engaged consumers are more likely to provide referrals or recommendations to others, which enhances the marketing efforts of the brand (Brodie et al. 2011) and results in long-term benefits such as increased brand reputation and equity (Van Doorn et al. 2010). Other examples of brand benefits from consumer engagement include increased sales, word-of-mouth recommendations, and consumer collaboration (Hollebeek, Glynn, and

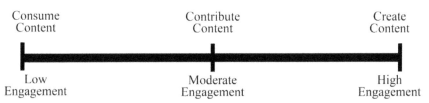

Figure 3.3:   Engagement Continuum. Courtesy of the author

Brodie 2014) as well as increased consumer loyalty, satisfaction, trust, and connection with the brand (Brodie et al. 2011).

Evaluating Cognitive/Affective Dimensions of Engagement

Similar to the behavioral approach to engagement, the overall model for the cognitive/affective approach was also found to be a statistically significant predictor of self-brand connection, loyalty, and fan-team relationship, and as previously discussed has potential to influence self-brand connection and the overall fan-team relationship more than behavioral dimensions. It was, however, the affective engagement dimension that was found to have a consistent influence across all variables. Furthermore, the beta values (see table C.1, appendix C) indicate that affective engagement has a moderate influence on self-brand connection and fan-team relationship. What this finding points to is that the affective, or positive emotions surrounding the use of Twitter to engage with a brand, is a key indicator of successful fan-team relationships. And based on the observed values, it has perhaps the strongest influence of any other dimension of engagement investigated in this study.

A commonly cited step for developing a consumer-brand relationship is to establish an emotional connection with the consumer (Arvidsson 2006). Emotions play a role in everyday decision-making. Morgan-Thomas and Veloutsou (2013) put it this way: "[F]eelings matter: consumers affectively bond with specific brands to form brand relationships" (21). Berry (2000) suggests "great brands transcend specific product features and benefits and

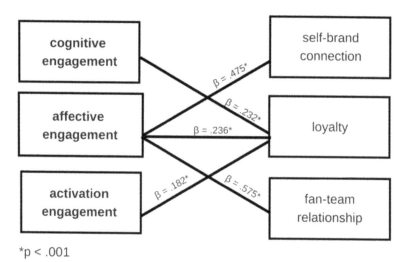

*p < .001

Figure 3.4:   Cognitive/Affective Dimensions of Engagement. Courtesy of the author

penetrate people's emotions" (134). Emotions are especially important for service-based brands that depend on continued patronage from consumers (Underwood, Bond, and Baer 2001). As consumers become emotionally attached to the brand, they tend to speak up on behalf of the brand and choose it over competitors (Dwyer, Greenhalgh, and LeCrom 2015). Connecting with consumers on an emotional level goes beyond rational and economic decision making and encourages feelings of affinity and trust (Berry 2000).

Emotions play an especially important role in the development of consumer-brand relationships for sport brands. Sport brands leverage the emotional attachment that fans have with the team to instill an increased sense of loyalty among identified fans (Couvelaere and Richelieu 2005). This form of "emotional loyalty" can be developed through regular interactions between the team and fans (Gladden, Irwin, and Sutton 2001). Sport brands can enhance the fan-team relationship by (1) seeking ways to understand the consumer, (2) creating opportunities for interaction between the brand and the consumer, (3) rewarding customer loyalty, and (4) integrating marketing associations to maintain a consistent message across platforms (Gladden, Irwin, and Sutton 2001).

CONCLUSION

Online engagement with a brand, can be beneficial for the consumer and the brand, as evidenced by the research presented within this chapter. Results of the research indicate three key takeaways related to using online engagement to facilitate relationship-building efforts. First, these data provide general support for engagement on Twitter as a useful relationship-building tool. To date few studies have made a direct connection between how users engage on social media and specific brand-related outcomes. Results of this study indicate that both behavioral and cognitive/affective dimensions of engagement can have a positive influence on not only the fan-team relationship, but also loyalty and the self-brand connection with the team. Related, the second takeaway is that research on online engagement needs to take a more comprehensive approach to measuring engagement. This study drew on two approaches to engagement—as a multidimensional behavioral construct and as a multidimensional cognitive/affective construct—to determine to what extent online engagement can help facilitate the fan-team relationship. It is suggested that scholars consider these two approaches in tandem for future online engagement research. Finally, two dimensions of engagement were consistently found to significantly and positively influence fan-team relationship—affective engagement and consuming content branded content using Twitter. Affective engagement represents the emotional connection the consumer has with the brand through online brand interactions. An emotional connection with a brand has long been cited as a key factor in all kinds of relationships. The emotional connection is particularly relevant in the sport context where fans often identify with the brand to the extent that it becomes part of their identity. As results of this study indicate, heightening that emotional connection can be an effective relationship-building strategy for sport brands.

Understandably the capability of immediate, two-way communication between consumers and brands constitutes much of the rationale for using Twitter as a relationship-building tool. However as demonstrated by this study, perhaps it is time to reconsider this. To date several studies have noted that most organizations are not utilizing the two-way communication features of social media (see Levenshus 2010; Waters and Williams 2011; Watkins 2016). Similarly, using experimental methods Watkins (2017) found that one-way communication methods using Twitter were effective for developing relationships between athletes and fans using Twitter. Similarly, the prevalence of consuming tweets or reading tweets as an effective indicator of fan-team relationships provides further support for the consideration of providing quality content more so than trying to encourage user-generated content.

Sport brands benefit from having a highly identified fan base, and as such, should invest in communicating relevant brand messages to fans that resonate with consumers on multiple levels (Karjaluoto, Munnukka, and Salmi 2016). As such, it is important to analyze the types of content created by sport brands to better understand what kind of content sport fans consume, thus providing the justification for the research reported in the next section of this book. This research supports online engagement through Twitter as an effective relationship-building tool, and more specifically reading tweets is one of the most effective forms of engagement, so it is natural then to need to evaluate what content sport fans consume.

Part Two

CONTENT STRATEGIES AND RELATIONSHIP MARKETING

The nature of sport as a service brand, and its dependence on fans for support, means that sport brands must develop marketing strategies that build, enhance, and maintain a positive relationship with fans. Developing a better understanding of the psychological processes that underlie fandom, team identification, and loyalty are important for sport brands. Knowing the attitudes and behaviors of committed fans can provide brand managers with insight into how to better present the sport product, effectively communicate with fans, and predict fan consumption behavior (Fink, Trail, and Anderson 2002; Funk and James 2006). Research in sports communication suggests that team and fan identification can be strengthened by strategic communication efforts from the team (Heere and James 2007); and as such, the goal of this section is to investigate social media strategies sport teams implement on social media that enhance identification, engagement, and ultimately the fan-team relationship.

The idea underpinning the relevance of engagement for strategic social media is that engaged consumers are valuable for brands because they are more motivated to seek out a relationship with the brand (Hollebeek, Glynn, and Brodie 2014). Research presented in this in part I of this book provided support for this assertion—online engagement using Twitter can be an effective tool for building fan-team relationships. This is consistent with the assertions made by proponents of relationship marketing for service-based brands—maintaining relationships with consumers provide a competitive advantage for brands (Van Doorn et al. 2010). Often, consumers who are motivated to engage with a brand are also willing to engage in a relationship with the brand (Gummerus et al. 2012). Continued online engagement between the consumer and brand should serve to strengthen the relationship between the consumer and the brand, or in the sport context the fans and team

(Men and Tsai 2014). As such, teams can develop social media content that furthers the relationship marketing efforts of the team.

RELATIONSHIP MARKETING

Relationship marketing represents a paradigm shift in marketing, away from a focus on the 4 P's (product, price, promotion, and place) to a focus on establishing relationships with customers (Gronroos 2004). Relationship marketing is defined as "attracting, maintaining, and in multi-service organizations enhancing customer relationships" (Berry 1995, 236), and was established on the assumption that it is more cost effective and efficient to retain existing customers than to attract new customers (Kim and Trail 2011; Stavros, Pope, and Winzar 2008). Relationships are maintained by exchanging and fulfilling promises made by both the consumer and the brand (Gronroos 2004). At its most basic level, relationship marketing is about retaining customers through building mutually beneficial and collaborative consumer-brand relationships (Abeza and O'Reilly 2014; Abeza, O'Reilly, and Reid 2013; Bee and Kahie 2006).

Relationship marketing represents a more flexible approach to marketing based on relational management rather than transactions (Cousens, Babiak, and Slack 2001). Communication is essential to the relationship marketing process, and brands should seek to have "interactive, individualized, and valued added contacts" throughout the life of the relationship (Shani 1997, 11). The consumer-focused approach of relationship marketing assumes the relationship between consumers and brands increases the overall value of the service being offered (Gronroos 2004).

Sport brands provide a unique context for studying relationship marketing techniques because consuming the sport product is a social process where a person can interact with other fans, athletes, and representatives of the team (Stavros and Westberg 2009). It was Shani (1997) who first proposed a framework for sport teams to incorporate relationship marketing into a sport brand's marketing strategy. The proposed framework provided a set of guidelines for moving the sport brand away from a more one-way traditional marketing strategy to a relationship marketing strategy. Using effective relationship marketing strategies allows the sport brand to develop a lasting bond with sport fans (Gray and Wert-Gray 2012). To engage in effective relationship marketing strategies, sport brands should seek to understand fan motivations to improve the quality of the consumer-brand relationship (Kim and Trail 2011; Stavros et al. 2014). To do so, sport brands should first determine what elements of the sport brand resonate most with sport fans, and then develop marketing strategies that enhance those elements (Bodet and Bernache-Assollant 2011).

Using relationship marketing, service providers can get to know and better meet the needs of the consumer (Berry 1995). Brands can tailor services to consumers to create a high-quality experience, which in turn leads to customer retention and increased brand loyalty (Abeza, O'Reilly, and Reid 2013). This is especially relevant for sport brands where factors including globalization, increased television coverage of sporting event, new technology, and increased sport market research has led to the adoption of relationship marketing techniques (Cousens, Babiak, and Slack 2001; Stavros, Pope, and Winzar 2008).

The end goal of relationship marketing is to retain customers by creating a sense of brand loyalty among consumers (Shani 1997). Brand loyalty is repeat buying behavior that results from favorable beliefs and attitudes toward the brand (Keller 1993). Loyal fans can become brand ambassadors who promote the brand to others (Bhattacharya and Sen 2003) and increases the overall brand equity for the team (Kaynak, Salman, and Tatoglu 2008). High levels of loyalty and involvement among consumers of a brand make the brand look more attractive to others thereby enhancing the likelihood that others will also choose to identify with the brand (Underwood, Bond, and Baer 2001).

PART TWO OVERVIEW

This section of the book is about analyzing social media content strategies sport brands employ to connect with consumers and enhance the fan-team relationship. When using social media as an integrated marketing communication tool, it is the brand's responsibility to initiate the relationship and create content that encourages consumer engagement (Culnan, McHugh, and Zubillag 2010). This chapter reports findings of research examining the Twitter content created by sport teams. Much of the existing research on social media for branding and marketing focus on categorizing content using general, prescribed categories. This research takes a different approach by using a thematic analysis to look more closely at how social media content can encourage increased levels of online engagement among consumers. Examining brand content on social media provides insight into how brands approach using social media as a relationship-building tool.

A thematic analysis of tweets produced by twelve teams representing the top four U.S. based professional sport leagues (Major League Baseball, MLB; National Basketball Association; NBA; National Football League, NFL; and National Hockey League, NHL) were analyzed. Using the Sport

Illustrated "Social 100" list as a guide, the top three teams from each league was selected for inclusion in this study. Teams included in the analysis include: (1) Seattle Mariners (MLB), (2) Houston Astros (MLB), (3) San Francisco Giants (MLB), (4) Atlanta Hawks (NBA), (5) Golden State Warriors (NBA), (6) Dallas Mavericks (NBA), (7) Carolina Panthers (NFL), (8) Arizona Cardinals (NFL), (9) Atlanta Falcons (NFL), (10), Los Angeles Kings (NHL), (11) Dallas Stars (NHL), and (12) Columbus Blue Jackets (NHL). Tweets were collected in June of 2017, and the last 200 tweets from each team was used in the analysis resulting in a total of 2,400 tweets.

Data was collected using Nvivo. The nCapture feature was used to collect the entire Twitter feed for each team in the analysis. Tweets were then sorted by date and only the latest 200 tweets were used in the analysis. Tweets were exported into an Excel document for analysis, thus creating a verbatim copy of the tweets, which included a link to the original tweet in the event that examination of a picture or graphic was necessary.

The researcher reviewed all the tweets to increase familiarity with the data (Lindlof and Taylor 2011) before starting the open coding stage of the data analysis. Open coding occurs when the researcher examines the data "for salient categories of information" that are supported by the data (Cresswell 2007, 160). The unit of analysis for this study was the tweet. During open coding labels were assigned to the data but the data was not categorized. During the next phase, axial coding, categorization of the data began. During the axial coding stage data was "played" with through grouping, deleting, editing, and merging open codes. Themes were determined according to Owen's (1984) guidelines: recurrence, repetition, and forcefulness. Axial coding continued until theoretical saturation occurred and no new themes emerged from the data (Strauss and Corbin 1998). The final stage of the analysis included interpretation where data is transformed to create new meaning (Coffey and Atkinson 1996). Different theoretical perspectives were used to guide this stage of the data analysis (see chapters 4 through 6).

Chapter 4

Brand Personality

An aspect of sport branding that is often overlooked is the challenge of working within a homogenous sport marketplace. Many teams make up a sports league, but ultimately all of these teams produce the same product. To illustrate this point, let's take Major League Baseball (MLB) for example. The MLB is made up of thirty teams in cities across the United States and Canada. The end goal for all of these teams is to win games and the World Series. In essence, all thirty sport brands (i.e., teams) that make up the MLB market do the same thing and offer the same product (i.e., a competitive sports team). A new MLB fan may have a hard time deciding which of the thirty teams that offer the same product they want to adopt as their team. This is where a brand's personality comes into play.

Brand personality is "a set of human characteristics associated with a brand" (Aaker 1997, 347). Brand personality is useful for differentiating brands in a crowded marketplace (Ross 2008; Watkins and Gonzenbach 2013). This is an important concept for all brands, including sport brands, that operate in homogenous markets. Furthermore, researchers have identified brand personality as a key factor for relationship building. Brand personality is important for establishing an emotional connection with the brand (Biel 1993) and allows the consumer to express him or herself through association with the brand (Carlson, Donavan, and Cumiskey 2009).

This chapter explores the concept of brand personality and the role it plays in helping to distinguish the sport brand and further fan-team relationship-building efforts. What follows is an overview of the concept of brand personality and how it has been studied in a sport context. Findings from a thematic analysis of tweets from professional sport teams reveal how teams communicate brand personality using Twitter. Implications for relationship-building strategies using social media are discussed.

BRAND PERSONALITY OVERVIEW

Before getting into the specifics of brand personality, it is beneficial to examine the overall concept of personality. Personality is "the unique psychological characteristics that lead to relatively consistent and lasting responses to one's own environment" (Kim, Lee, and Lee 2008, 9). A personality is made up of various traits. Trait theory was developed to explain how these traits make up a person's personality. Human personality is a complex mechanism often defined by a set of multiple traits rather than just a single trait that frequently reinforce or contradict one another (McCrae and Costa 1995). It is the combination of these traits that guide human behavior and make up personality (Kim, Lee, and Lee 2008, 9; McCrae and Costa 1995). Personality traits influence the motives and attitudes that ultimately lead to behavioral changes (McCrae and Costa 1995).

As previously discussed, brand personality is the attribution of human qualities to a brand (Aaker 1997). Unlike humans, brands are inanimate objects; therefore, personality traits must be projected onto the brand (Kim, Lee, and Lee 2008; Heere 2010). Carlson and Donavan (2013) explain, "brand personality is a dynamic amalgamation of unique attributes (i.e., brand adjectives) working together to create an overall personality for the brand" (196). Much like an organization's brand image, brand personality is communicated through brand identity (Kim, Magnusen, and Kim 2012), and consumer perception of brand personality is a confirmation of that brand identity (Heere 2010). Therefore, creating brand personality is two-fold. First, the brand must develop strategic communication tactics that communicate aspects of the brand personality, and second, it is ultimately the consumer and their perception of the brand that either confirms or rejects the personality.

Brand personality is largely dependent on consumer experience with the brand (Aaker 1997; Patterson 1999). In this sense, brand personality can be considered "the way in which a consumer perceives the brand on dimensions that typically capture a person's personality extended to the domain of brands," (Batra, Lehmann, and Singh 1993, 83). A sport brand has a number of tools to communicate brand personality, which will be discussed later, but a key point to remember for now is that brand personality depends on consumer perception.

Brand Personality and Sports

The sport brand personality often takes on the image of the administration, team and fans and by traits the team exhibits through its marketing and style of play (Tsiotsou 2012). The complexity of brand personality is largely determined by the traits a sports organization exhibits through its marketing and style of play. Taken together, these elements create a complex and dynamic brand personality. As such, scholars have worked to better understand the dynamics of sport brand personality. Studies have attempted to develop brand personality scales specific to sports (Braunstein and Ross 2010; Kang 2015; Schade, Piehler, and Burmann 2014; Tsiotsou 2012). Other studies have looked at the personality of athlete endorsers (Boyd and Shank 2004; Braunstein and Zhang 2005; Carlson and Donavan 2013). More specifically, studies have revealed that the unique personality of athletes can influence consumer perception. When consumers identify with an athlete, then they are more likely to form attachments with the team and purchase team-related products (Carlson and Donavan 2013). Furthermore, brand personality attributes can influence identification with a sport team, which ultimately leads to increased purchase behavior (Carlson and Donavan 2013).

MEASURING BRAND PERSONALITY

Researchers have identified five basic dimensions of personality, commonly referred to as the "Big Five" (Aaker 1997; Kim, Lee, and Lee 2008). These personality traits are extraversion, agreeableness, conscientiousness, neuroticism, and openness to experience. These traits are commonly accepted as being descriptive of human personality, but there is not as much agreement about the traits of brand personality. Specific to consumer goods, five dimensions of brand personality have been identified: sincerity, excitement, competence, sophistication, and ruggedness (Aaker 1997).

In a sport context, studies found the original brand personality scale was not applicable to sport and suggested that researchers develop a sport-specific brand personality scale (Ross 2008). Building on this research, Tsiotsou (2012) developed a brand personality scale using the traits competitiveness, prestige, morality, authenticity, and credibility. Likewise, Schade, Piehler, and Burmann (2014) published a second scale measuring sport brand personality based on four personality traits: extraversion, rebellious, open-mindedness, and conscientiousness.

Despite these efforts, there is not a consensus among sport researchers about how to determine brand personality for sport brands. This lead some researchers to suggest that related to sport brands a different approach is required (Carlson and Donavan 2013). The argument is that rather than being "trait based" like human personality, a brand personality is "state based" (Carlson and Donavan 2013, 196). A personality state is "temporary, brief, and caused by external circumstances" (Carlson and Donavan 2013, 196). The assumption that brand personality is largely determined by consumer perception of a brand based on interaction and experience with the brand, makes the state-based approach to brand personality a more logical argument.

Sports marketers should develop marketing strategies that are consistent with the intended brand image, but as the team's situation changes then marketers need to adjust marketing efforts to reflect the personality state of the team at that time. For example, let's say a team has experienced a run of bad luck and has not advanced to the playoffs in several years. This team may be overlooked by the media and the public, but add a star player and new coach, and injects some excitement into the team and the image starts to change to reflect the new look of the team. In other words, allow the brand personality to evolve with the team. As this new-look team starts to gain more success and a distinct playing identity, then brand personality of the team should evolve as well.

DEVELOPING BRAND PERSONALITY IN SPORTS

It was established earlier that sport teams operate in a homogenous market, with all teams in a league producing the same product. For sports, one way that a team can distinguish itself from others is through its team building and style of play (Carlson, Donavan, and Cumiskey 2009). As such, one can look at style of play as one factor that contributes to the development of a team's brand personality. Let's look at a key sports rivalry in the early 1990s as an example—the NBA's Los Angeles Lakers and the Detroit Pistons. While these two teams had epic on-the-court battles, the two teams couldn't have been more different in terms of its perceived brand personality. The Los Angeles Lakers, who earned the nickname Showtime Lakers, used its proximity to Hollywood and the entertainment industry and a flashy style of play by enigmatic players like Earvin "Magic" Johnson and Kareem Abdul-Jabbar to develop a team personality that indicated excitement for fans. This stood in direct contrast to the Pistons who proudly wore the nickname "Bad Boy Pistons." Lead by Isaiah Thomas, Bill Laimbeer, Rick Mahorn, and Dennis Rodman, this team and style of play reflected the blue-collar roots of its home city of Detroit. The style of play and personality for each of these teams, who played during roughly the same time period, was drastically different and appealed to different sets of fans.

The brand personality communicated through the style of play can be carried over into the marketing of the team (Watkins and Gonzenbach 2013). Other factors that contribute to the development of brand personality for the team includes team success, brand identity, visual identity cues, and fan interactions with the team (Braunstein and Ross 2010; Phillips, McQuarrie, and Griffin 2014; Ross 2008). Therefore, the strategy the organization uses to communicate the brand image to the public is imperative to the development of the brand's personality (Plummer 2000).

THEMATIC ANALYSIS RESULTS

Findings of the analysis of tweets from professional sport teams revealed three strategies for communicating brand personality on Twitter: (1) differentiating the brand, (2) personality congruence, and (3) enhancing the fan-team connection. The following sections report the findings of this analysis and provide insights into how fans react to these strategies.

Differentiating the Brand

As previously discussed, on the surface there is not much that differentiates one sport brand from another. Sport brands must rely on different factors that distinguish it from other teams in the league. One way to distinguish one brand from another is by creating unique brand associations. Brand associations are components of a brand that are linked to a brand and provide meaning for the consumer. Brand associations are used to "differentiate, position, and extend brands, to create positive attitudes and feelings toward brands" and as such, can communicate aspects of a brand's personality (Low and Lamb 2000, 351). By highlighting team brand associations, fans are able to create additional associations with the team. As a result, the team's brand personality becomes more complex and fans are more likely to identify with and remain loyal to the team (Wallace, Wilson, and Miloch 2011).

Brand associations are developed through consumer interactions with a brand, and the experiential nature of sports allows for a wide range of brand associations (Gladden and Funk 2002). To further the distinctiveness of the sport brand, marketers can create advertisements, including social media content, that features images of players making exciting plays that highlight the physical intensity of the game (Gladden and Funk 2002). Still other sport brands may benefit from focusing on attributes outside of playing style, such as team history, home arena, or unique fan traditions. The idea is to focus messages on the traits that differentiate one team from another and incorporate that into the team's brand personality. Teams can use social media to accomplish this by incorporating unique elements of its visual identity into social media content, developing a distinct online voice, and utilizing brand associations into the content such as mascots and cheerleaders.

Results of the analysis found that professional sport brands used Twitter to highlight a variety of brand associations including mentions of the team mascot's exploits: "Beat Bailey's 23 squats! Post your video with

#FitToBeKing to win prizes from @24hourfitness and Lenny & Larry's" (#LAKings[1]); information about the team's home venue: "Experience a behind-the-scenes tour of the Hawks' locker room. RSVP now" (Atlanta Hawks[2]); and the team's cheerleaders and dance team: "GALLERY: Photos from Week 3 of @MavsDancers prep classes! #DMDAuditions are less than a month away" (Dallas Mavericks[3]). These tweets provide fans with brand touchpoints with the team beyond the actual sport and athlete. The more complex and varied the brand associations, then the more distinct the sport brand.

Another brand association that is particularly important in the sport context is team jerseys and t-shirts. At the time of data collection, the National Hockey League (NHL) unveiled new team jerseys, and teams used this as an opportunity to encourage fans to purchase the new merchandise. For example, the LA Kings tweeted: "*checks closet* *sees 13 LA Kings jerseys* 'Yup, gonna need the new one'" (#LAKings[4]). The Columbus Blue Jackets also used Twitter to get fans excited about the new jersey design: "TOMORROW! We're ready, @adidasHockey. #CBJ" which included a ten-second teaser video for the new jersey (Columbus Blue Jackets[5]). Whereas, the Dallas Stars appealed to fans by highlighting what distinguishes the new jersey from the older versions: "It's not all about looks. See how our new @addidashockey jersey is different from the previous version" (Dallas Stars[6]).

Jerseys were not the only form of merchandise to receive attention on Twitter. Other teams used Twitter to tell fans about merchandise giveaways. The Columbus Blue Jackets tweeted, "WE HAVE #BOB4VEZINA BUTTONS! Come and find us! #CBJ" (ColumbusBlueJackets[7]). Still other teams used Twitter to announce merchandise sales. For example, the Dallas Mavericks retweeted information about a 50% off Spring Clearance sale for Mavericks gear (Mavgear.com[8]). The Houston Astros used a free t-shirt giveaway to get fans to engage online: "Want one of these awesome #VoteAstros t-shirts? Reply to this tweet with your #VoteAstros maxed-out ballot for a chance to win" (Houston Astros[9]).

Wearing team t-shirts and jerseys is an important ritual. It allows sport fans to publicly demonstrate their identification with the team, but beyond that, it represents a feeling of belonging with the group. Research has found that highly identified sport fans are more likely to spend time and money following the team (Dwyer, Greenhalgh, and LeCrom 2015; Meng, Stavros, and Westberg 2015). From a brand perspective, the jerseys and merchandise associated with a team are designed specifically for that brand including branded colors and logos, which can be a signifier of a team's brand personality. As such, it is a good idea for sport brands to encourage fans to purchase and wear merchandise affiliated with the team. Using social media to generate excitement for new merchandise, and notifications for when merchandise is on sale, is an important branding strategy for sport teams.

Personality Congruence

Relationships between brands and consumers, or sport brands and fans, is similar to the process of developing a relationship between two people (Carlson, Donavan, and Cumiskey 2009; Fournier 1998). A personality, even a brand's perceived personality, can play an important role in the strengthening of a consumer-brand relationship (Aaker, Fournier, and Braseal 2004; Carlson and Donavan 2013; Nobre, Becker, and Brito 2010). When we seek out relationships with other people, we often look for things that we may have in common with the other person, and perhaps most importantly, we look for someone with whom we have a compatible personality. Personality congruence is just as important in consumer-brand relationships as it is in our interpersonal relationships (Kim, Lee, and Lee 2008), and as a result, "sports fans may gravitate towards teams to be associated with their defining personality characteristics" (Carlson, Donavan, and Cumiskey 2009, 373).

Consumers look for congruency in brand personality (Aaker 1997; Donavan, Carlson, and Zimmerman 2005), or brands that they feel reflect their own personality. The more consumers perceive a brand to match their own personality (or their ideal personality), then the more likely they are to form an emotional attachment to the brand (Swaminathan, Stilley, and Ahluwalia 2008). A sport team with a unique brand personalities could have a significant influence on identification with a team (Carlson, Donavan, and Cumiskey 2009). Therefore, it is important for sport teams to communicate a brand personality that is not only distinct from other teams, but also resonates with the fans.

It is important for brands, especially sport brands, to understand the fans' perception of the brand in order to develop messages that align the organization's personality traits (Braunstein and Ross 2010). One of the interesting findings to emerge from the analysis was the ways in which sport brands used the language and features of social media to create relatable social media content for fans in order to highlight the personality congruence with fans. Results of the Twitter analysis revealed that professional sport brands used features such as memes, references to popular culture, holidays, and current events to create content that was relevant to fans beyond sports.

Memes

Memes are defined as "a cultural unit (e.g., an idea, value, or pattern of behavior) that is passed from one person to another in social settings" (Xie et al. 2011, 297). Memes are a frequent feature of social media content, and increasingly make their way into the offline world. Most online memes take the form of a picture of graphic with accompanying text. Other forms of memes include the use of popular phrases in social media content. Both the Atlanta Hawks and Arizona Cardinals used the hashtag meme #FirstGifComesUpForYourName in a tweet, accompanied by a GIF of an athlete from the team (Atlanta Hawks[10] and Arizona Cardinals[11]). The inclusion of memes into social media content shows that the sport brand is up-to-date with trends and the language of social media.

Popular Culture

References to popular culture in tweets also help to humanize the image of the sport brand. The Dallas Mavericks posted a tweet with the copy "Need something to get you through Monday?? Here you go!" (Dallas Mavericks[12]), which included a short video of players lip synching to the popular song "Can't Stop the Feeling" by Justin Timberlake. The Seattle Mariners and San Francisco Giants hosted a "Game of Thrones" night and to promote the event, each team tweeted *Game of Thrones* references including the popular tagline for the show, "Winter is Coming" (Mariners[13]). The San Francisco Giants personalized the tweet with a branded hashtag #HouseOfPence in reference to the different houses on the show and one of the team's franchise players, Hunter Pence (San Francisco Giants[14]). Incorporating popular culture references into social media demonstrates that team is relevant with what is going on in culture beyond just sports, and as such, provides an additional touchpoint for fans to relate to the team.

Holidays and Current Events

In addition to memes and popular culture references, all sport brands in the analysis made reference to holidays. All twelve brands in the sample tweeted about how players celebrated Father's Day. The Columbus Blue Jackets tweeted a link to a story about how their players celebrate Father's Day (Columbus Blue Jackets[15]). Likewise, the @DallasStars tweeted, "Part-time hockey players, full-time Dads. #HappyFathersDay!" (Dallas Stars[16])" featuring a graphic of a player with his children. Other sport brands took a more fan-oriented approach. For example, the Atlanta Falcons tweeted, "Thank you for teaching us the game and creating countless memories that will last forever, Dad. #RiseUp" (Atlanta Falcons[17]), and the Arizona Cardinals, "We figured all the dads out there needed one more 'No. 1 Dad' shirt! Happy #FathersDay!" including a picture of a Cardinals jersey with a #1 and Dad for the name (Arizona Cardinals[18]).

Another recent trend that is attributable to social media, is the less traditional holidays. These includes days like #NationalSelfieDay, #NationalDonutDay, or #NationalSunglassesDay. The Golden State Warriors, coming off a finals win, tweeted, "#NationalSelfieDay #DubNation" including a selfie of players during the championship parade (GoldenStateWarriors[19]).

Sport brands in the analysis used holidays and current events to encourage fans engagement with the team. For Father's Day, the LA Kings used the holiday to encourage fans to upload pictures using the team app. The team tweeted, "Post a picture of your hockey dad and you could be featured in our Father's Day collage!" (#LAKings[20]) followed by a link with instructions. Similarly, the San Francisco Giants encouraged fans to upload selfies wearing their Giants hat with a promise to retweet some of the favorites (San Francisco Giants[21]). Tweets using these tactics are able to serve two purposes—first, they keep the brand involved in the conversation of the day, and second, they provide a natural outlet to get fans involved with the brand beyond sports.

These tweets exemplify the various ways that sport brands are using the features and language of social media to create content that is relatable to fans. Incorporating memes and popular culture references into their Twitter content allows sport brands to ingratiate themselves into internet culture, thus making the sport brand more relatable. Through creating relatable social media content, sport brands are able to "personify brands and help build and maintain consumer relationships by engaging in conversations" (Kwon and Sung 2011, 5). Relatable content is imbued with personality and helps consumers further their connection with a brand by projecting values, traits, and emotions on the brand (Patterson 1999). The more the consumer finds their values and personality aligning with the brand, then the more likely the consumer is to connect with the brand on a personal level (Carlson and Donavan 2013).

Enhancing the Fan-Team Connection

Consuming the sport product is an experiential process. As a result, a person's perception of a team's brand personality is likely to be influenced by their interactions and experiences with the team (Ross 2008). Most people come in contact with the sport brand through attending and watching games on TV, or more recently, following the team on social media. Brands with a strong social media presence are better equipped to capture consumer attention, receive feedback from consumers, and increase overall brand awareness. Likewise, fans who supplement traditional media with social media to follow sports are likely to spend more time interacting with the team (Walsh et al. 2013). This increased exposure to the team-related messaging can have a greater impact on the fan's perception of the team's brand personality.

Social media is a storytelling platform. It is not about pushing sales on consumers, but rather, it is designed to share stories. Brands that are successful on social media have recognized this and implemented it into their social strategy. Advertisers have long valued and emphasized the importance of using stories to establish an emotional connection with audiences. This same principle is relevant to creating social media content. Sport brands should tell stories that not only reflect the team's personality, but also sparks an emotional connection with fans. Results of the Twitter analysis found three story themes that teams used to spark an emotional connection with fans—team history, togetherness and family, and hard work.

Team History

Sport teams posted tweets that relayed some aspect of the team's history. For example, the Arizona Cardinals posted, "On this day in 1903, Ernie Nevers was born. Nevers scored 40 points in a game in 1929, which is still the @ NFL single-game record" (Arizona Cardinals[22]), and the Atlanta Hawks posted, "On this day in 1993, Lenny Wilkens was named our head coach #tbt" (Atlanta Hawks[23]). Communicating the history of the team is another strategy for brand differentiation (Watkins 2014a). Incorporating information about the team's history on social media creates additional brand associations with the team, which can influence perceptions of the team. Subsequently, this can be positive for the brand (Underwood, Bond, and Baer 2001). A team's history is unique to the team, and is influenced by the location, players, and personalities associated with the team. Thus, history can become a key factor in enhancing fan identification with a team (Richelieu and Pons 2009; Wann 2006), which is important for the development of fan-team relationships.

Togetherness and Family

Several tweets from sport teams across leagues created Twitter content that focused on belonging or being part of the team. The Atlanta Falcons tweeted, "The Brotherhood is only getting stronger," which featured a short video of the team participating in offseason organized team activities (e.g., OTAs; Atlanta Falcons[24]). Likewise, during the 2016–2017 NBA Playoffs, the Golden State Warriors incorporated the branded hashtag #StrengthInNumbers in order to communicate the role of the fans as being an important part of the team's playoff run. The tweet was accompanied by a short video titled "Strength in Numbers: For the Bay" (Golden State Warriors[25]). This video featured images of the team, the Bay Area, and fans with a chant of "Warriors" in the background. The Carolina Panthers also paid homage to their hometown by posting a tweet that read "Home. #OneCarolina" accompanied by a picture of the Charlotte city skyline (Carolina Panthers[26]). Tweeting about togetherness and family reiterates the us versus them aspect that is prevalent in sports. Social identification with a sport team is about finding a place to belong and with these tweets, teams are reinforcing that message for fans.

Hard Work

Sport brands communicated with fans that players were hard at work during the offseason to improve and be ready for the next season. The Dallas Mavericks tweeted, "@swish 41 is more than ready to assist the Mavs in whatever capacity is needed this summer" (Dallas Mavericks[27]). This tweet, referring to the team's franchise player, Dirk Nowitzki, is followed by a sponsored report that keeps fans up-to-date on how the team preparations for next season are progressing. Another tweet from the Dallas Mavericks features a newer player to the team: "Nerlens Noel loves Dallas and is getting a head start on summer workouts with his teammates!" (Dallas Mavericks[28]) followed by a link to a full article about the athlete. Similarly, the Atlanta Falcons also highlighted the team's preparations for next season: "Getting better every day" (Atlanta Falcons[29]), which was followed by a link to a photo gallery of pictures from OTAs. Through these tweets, teams reminded fans that the team was focused on a goal and was working to achieve this goal. This kind of news can help fans get excited for the upcoming season.

In addition to differentiating a brand and promoting consumer-brand congruence, a brand's personality can also resonate with the consumer on an emotional level, which can enhance identification, and ultimately the fan's relationship with the team. A brand personality that resonates with a consumer can spark an emotional connection that can strengthen their relationship with the brand by evoking feelings and brand associations for the consumer (Biel 1993). An emotional connection with a brand has been found to have positive benefits for the brand including increased brand loyalty and brand equity (Freling, Crosno, and Henard 2011). Based on the findings of this study, the use of the storytelling function among teams is useful for communicating brand personality, and can lead to identification with a team.

CONCLUSION

Sport brands carry symbolic meaning for many fans, including community pride, socialization, achievement, and identification of role models (Kang 2015). Brand personality is one way that teams can personify that symbolic meaning. Through the process of applying a brand personality to a sports team, sport fans develop a more active role in the relationship (Biel 1993). At this point, once the connection between the fan and the team has been made, the team must maintain communication and provide opportunities for interaction between the fan and the team in order to strengthen the relationship. Thus, from this perspective, the perceived brand personality of a sports team can be thought of as a catalyst for initiating the relationship between the fan and the team.

In addition to relationship building, developing a strong and unique brand personality can result in other benefits for the sports organization. Research suggests that unique brand associations, including brand personality, can have positive effects for a brand's overall equity or value (Freling, Crosno, and Henard 2011; Keller 1993). Creating unique brand associations is essential for developing consumer-based brand equity (Walsh et al. 2013). Customer-based brand equity is "a set of brand assets and liabilities that add or subtract from the value provided by a product or service to a firm and/or to that firm's customers" (Freling, Crosno, and Henard 2011, 393). Additionally, a distinct brand personality can have financial benefits for a sports brand (Walsh et al. 2013), and by promoting an attractive image, sport brands can increase the number of games watched and retail spending among fans (Carlson, Donavan, and Cumiskey 2009).

Results of the analysis of Twitter activity revealed three ways brand personality was used to connect with fans. First, brand personality is useful for differentiating the team brand from other brands. This is especially important in the sport marketplace. Sport brands used Twitter to communicate its brand personality and enhance fan identification by creating content that contained unique brand associations, such as the home venue or mascots. In particular, featuring jerseys and merchandise sales is one way that teams distinguished its brand and encouraged fan involvement. Second, Twitter was used to communicate aspects of the team's brand personality that aligned with the fans using the language and features of social media. In particular, sport brands used memes, popular culture references, and current events, such as holidays, to create relatable content for fans. Finally, by telling stories about the team that elicited an emotional response from fans, the teams were able to enhance the connection fans had with the team.

While social media can be helpful to the development of brand personality, Nobre, Becker, and Brito (2010) cautions that it can also cause "rapid disruptions in a brand's image to occur for legitimate or irrational reasons" (212). In order for brand personality to be effective, it must be perceived favorably, clearly, and as original by the consumer (Freling, Crosno, and Henard 2011). Social media provides marketers with a medium for distributing and shaping its brand image and personality, but one of the defining features of Web 2.0 technologies like social media is the capability of user-generated content. Anyone can create content or engage in online discussions about a brand that is beyond the control of the brand manager. As previously discussed, brand personality is also attributed to a consumer's interactions with the brand—including online and offline interactions. Therefore, it is possible that a consumer's perception of a brand can be altered by these interactions.

NOTES

1. #LAKings [LAKings]. (2017, June 12). Beat Bailey's 23 squats! Post your video with #FitToBeKing to win prizes from @24hourfitness and Lenny & Larry's. http://LAKings.com/FTBKChallenge [Tweet]. Retrieved from https://twitter.com/i/web/status/874370736239947776

2. Atlanta Hawks [ATLHawks]. (2017, June 5). Experience a behind-the-scenes tour of the Hawks' locker room. RSVP Now: on.nba.com/2qR79VC [Tweet]. Retrieved from https://twitter.com/ATLHawks/status/871837787292565505/photo/1

3. Dallas Mavericks [dallasmavs]. (2017, June 20). GALLERY: Photos from Week 3 of @MavsDancers prep classes! #DMDAuditions are less than a month away! Go.mavs.com/I/5BC [Tweet]. Retrieved from https://twitter.com/i/web/status/877189973732200449

4. #LAKings [LAKings]. (2017, June 20). *checks closet* *sees 13 LA Kings jerseys* "Yup, gonna need the new one" [Tweet]. Retrieved from https://twitter.com/LAKings/status/877345449866215424/video/1

5. ColumbusBlueJackets [BlueJacketsNHL]. (2017, June 19). TOMORROW! We're ready, @adidasHockey. #CBJ. [Tweet]. Retrieved from https://twitter.com/BlueJacketsNHL/status/876854616121409538/video/1

6. Dallas Stars [DallasStars]. (2017, June 21). It's not all about looks. See how our new @adidashockey jersey is different from the previous version. Nhl.com/stars/fans/adi [Tweet]. Retrieved from https://twitter.com/i/web/status/877645639194218496

7. ColumbusBlueJackets [BlueJacketsNHL]. (2017, June 21). WE HAVE #BOB4VEZINA BUTTONS! Come and find us! #CBJ [Tweet]. Retrieved from https://twitter.com/BlueJacketsNHL/status/877607326127054848/photo/1

8. Mavgear.com [mavgear]. (2017, May 25). Last Chance to [sic] Up to 50% Off! The Spring Clearance Sale Ends Tonight! Bit.ly/2rDrH7F [Tweet]. Retrieved from https://twitter.com/mavgear/status/867756980500410368/photo/1

9. Houston Astros [astros]. (2017, June 20). Want one of these awesome #Vote Astros t-shirts? Reply to this tweet with your #VoteAstros maxed-out ballot for a chance to win! [Tweet]. Retrieved from https://twitter.com/i/web/status/877223360832442368

10. AtlantaHawks[ATLHawks].(2017,June20).#FirstGIFComesUpForYourName [Tweet]. Retrieved from https://twitter.com/ATLHawks/status/877158412366348288/photo/1

11. Arizona Cardinals [AZCardinals]. (2017, June 20). #FirstGIFComesUpForYourName [Tweet]. Retrieved from https://twitter.com/AZCardinals/status/877237562842112000/photo/1

12. Dallas Mavericks [dallasmavs]. (2017, May 22). Need something to get you through your Monday?? Here you go! [Tweet] Retrieved from https://twitter.com/dallasmavs/status/866681334751649794/video/1

13. Mariners [Mariners]. (2017, June 17). Winter is coming. Celebrate the return of @GameOfThrones with this Ticket Special on Tuesday. m.mlb.com/mariners/ticke [Tweet]. Retrieved from https://twitter.com/i/web/status/876280828543864832

14. San Francisco Giants [SFGiants]. (2017, June 21).@GameOfThrones Night is coming to SF on 7/20! #HouseOfPence Bobblehead: atmlb.com/2IX1lbr #GoTMLB #WeAreSF #WinterIsComing #SFGiants [Tweet]. Retrieved from https://twitter.com/i/web/status/877589453513998337

15. ColumbusBlueJackets [BlueJacketsNHL]. (2017, June 18). What father-hood is like for players on the #CBJ [Tweet]. Retrieved from https://twitter.com/BlueJacketsNHL/status/876551094868090884

16. Dallas Stars [DallasStars]. (2017, June 18). Part-time hockey players, full-time Dads. #HappyFathersDay! [Tweet]. Retrieved from https://twitter.com/DallasStars/status/876509606951911425/photo/1

17. Atlanta Falcons [AtlantaFalcons]. (2017, June 18). Thank you for teaching us the game and creating countless memories that will last forever, Dad. #RiseUp. [Tweet]. Retrieved from https://twitter.com/AtlantaFalcons/status/876439625534812160/photo/1

18. Arizona Cardinals [AZCardinals]. (2017, June 18). We figured all the dads out there needed one more "No. 1 Dad" shirt! Happy #FathersDay! [Tweet]. Retrieved from https://twitter.com/AZCardinals/status/876462023869030400/photo/1

19. GoldenStateWarriors [warriors]. (2017, June 21). #NationalSelfieDay #DubNation [Tweet]. Retrieved from https://twitter.com/warriors/status/877549428244189184/photo/1

20. #LAKings [LAKings]. (2017, June 13). Post a picture of your hockey dad and you could be featured in our Father's Day collage! vxl.me/FathersDay2017 [Tweet]. Retrieved from https://twitter.com/LAKings/status/874657643184267265/photo/1

21. San Francisco Giants [SFGiants]. (2017, June 21). Afternoon TO DO list: 1 Wear your #SFGiants cap 2 take a selfie 3 Tag us We'll RT some of our favorites! #NationalSelfieDay [Tweet]. Retrieved from https://twitter.com/i/web/status/877630714551779329

22. Arizona Cardinals [AZCardinals]. (2017, June 11). On This Day in 1903, Ernie Nevers was born. Nevers scored 40 points in a game in 1929, which is still the @ NFL single-game points record. [Tweet]. Retrieved from https://twitter.com/i/web/status/873932862910644224

23. Atlanta Hawks [ATLHawks]. (2017, June 1). On this day in 1993, Lenny Wilkens was named our head coach! #tbt [Tweet]. Retrieved from https://twitter.com/ATLHawks/status/870415413426872320/photo/1

24. Atlanta Falcons [AtlantaFalcons]. (2017, June 6). The Brotherhood is only getting stronger. [Tweet]. Retrieved from https://twitter.com/AtlantaFalcons/status/872079380784201728/video/1

25. GoldenStateWarriors [warriors]. (2017, June 12). Game 5 #StrengthInNumbers [Tweet]. Retrieved from https://twitter.com/warriors/status/874400952727371778/

26. Carolina Panthers [Panthers]. (2017, June 10). Home. #OneCarolina [Tweet]. Retrieved from https://twitter.com/Panthers/status/873550940858724353/photo/1

27. Dallas Mavericks [dallasmavs]. (2017, May 15). .@swish41 is more than ready to assist the Mavs in whatever capacity is needed this summer. @BBVACompass REPORT: go.mavs.com/l/5/mZ [Tweet]. Retrieved from https://twitter.com/i/web/status/864133297168801793

28. Dallas Mavericks [dallasmavs]. (2017, May 23). Nerlens Noel loves Dallas and is getting a head start on summer workouts with his teammates! READ MORE: go.mavs.com/l/5qB [Tweet]. Retrieved from https://twitter.com/dallasmavs/status/867064879898705920

29. Atlanta Falcons [AtlantaFalcons]. (2017, June 5). Getting better every day. OTA photos atlfal.co.nz/2rFclaQ [Tweet]. Retrieved from https://twitter.com/AtlantaFalcons/status/871914429042053120/photo/1

Chapter 5

Connecting with Athletes

When you watch team sports, do you watch your favorite team or favorite player? What happens to your attachment to a team when your favorite player is traded? These are questions that sport fans frequently have to grapple with in an age of free agency and trades. For example, in the summer of 2016, NBA star Kevin Durant, announced that he was leaving the Oklahoma City Thunder to join the Golden State Warriors. Durant, considered to be among the best players in the league, joined another historically great team who played in the finals the season before. As a result, there was much controversy about a star of Durant's caliber joining an already great team through free agency. The aftermath of this decision found many fans of Durant and the Thunder upset.

Outside of free agency, the decision for a player to stay with a team or to go to another team is often made at the executive level; nonetheless, these decisions have far-reaching implications beyond just building a roster. Player trades and free agency can also have implications for the team brand and ability to maintain relationships with fans. Fans burning jerseys after a star player leaves the team exemplifies the emotional connection that sport fans have with their favorite athletes and why athletes can be a key factor in the development of fan-team relationships. Fan identification with an athlete can be an indicator of future identification with a sport or team (Pegoraro 2010). Additionally, researchers have suggested that athletes have more influence over their fans than other celebrities (Hambrick et al. 2010).

This chapter examines the celebrity of professional athletes and how that celebrity and the attachment fans have with their favorite athletes helps enhance fan identification with a team. What follows is a discussion of the celebrity role of professional athletes, and how that role enhances identification with athletes and teams they represent. Drawing on parasocial interaction theory from communication literature, this chapter focuses on how the seemingly one-sided relationship between fans and athletes can translate to a relationship. Findings from a thematic analysis of tweets from professional sport teams reveal how they incorporate athletes into the Twitter content strategy. Implications for relationship building on social media are discussed.

ATHLETES AND CELEBRITY

The sport industry has evolved from playing a game to a professional entertainment enterprise (Braunstein and Zhang 2005). This enterprise includes personalities that can be characterized as heroes, villains, celebrities, and superstars (Summers and Morgan 2008). Sport media adds to this story by framing sporting events and the performance of athletes as high stakes, dramatic events (Sun 2010). Sport headlines include phrases like "All Time Greatest" and spur debates about who is the greatest athlete in a given sport. It is this drama that is essential for the commercialization of the sport product (Summers and Morgan 2008). As such, participants in the sport product, the athletes, stand to benefit personally and professionally from the star power generated by this type of notoriety (Braunstein and Zhang 2005).

The athlete as celebrity can be traced back to the "Golden Age" of sport media. Sport writers used descriptive language and rich imagery to create a "larger than life" image of athletes, which elevated athletes to celebrity status. A celebrity is "a social actor who maintains the ability to generate a significant amount of public attention and prompt positive emotional reactions from stakeholder audiences" (Agyemang and Williams 2016, 243). In a sport context, celebrity athletes are "individuals who achieve fame through the sports they play" (Hambrick and Mahoney 2011, 162). A person makes the leap from being a public figure to being a celebrity when their name not only attracts attention but can also generate a profit (Braunstein and Zhang 2005). This attention provides added value for the individual, which can be used to help the individual's team or sport (Williams et al. 2015).

Athletes lead lives that are exciting and different from that of the general public. Summers and Morgan (2008) put it this way:

> It is well known that the sport media relies on entertainment, drama, gossip, and great pictures for its survival. Sport celebrities provide the essential elements for the media machine through their regular live performances on the sporting field where the outcome of their efforts is largely uncontrollable and therefore exciting to the everyday consumer. (p. 178)

There is a difference between the athlete as sport hero and celebrity: "sports heroes are recognized for their athletic skills and outstanding accomplishments in high-level sport competitions; recognition for celebrity athletes is rooted in fame through media coverage" (Braunstein and Zhang 2005, 243). An athlete's performance on the field is important for creating awareness and generating attention, but it is what the athlete does off the field to enhance his or her brand equity that makes the person a celebrity (Pegoraro and Jinnah 2012). As such, athletes that reach celebrity status should carefully manage their brand, which often includes aspects of their careers and personal lives (Kristiansen and Williams 2015). Athletes typically turn to public relations agencies and publicists to manage their public persona. Sport fans are aware that the public image of athletes is frequently a construction of careful public relations and branding efforts (Summers and Morgan 2008).

THE CELEBRITY-FAN RELATIONSHIP

Parasocial interaction (PSI) provides an interesting theoretical framework for better understanding the relationship between fans and athletes. First developed from communication research, PSI examines the relationship between media users and media personalities (Labrecque 2014). PSI research was originally developed by Horton and Wohl (1956) and focuses on the relationship between television viewers and media personalities (Sun and Wu 2012). PSI is a "one-sided and mediated interaction that takes place between a media user and a media persona" (Frederick, Hambrick, and Clavio 2014, 4). PSI represents the perception of a relationship with a media personality (Sun 2010), and media users (or sport fans) express interest in learning more about the media persona as they would get to know a friend (Labrecque 2014). PSI has been applied to marketing research as a way to describe consumer-brand relationships. In this context, PSI is defined as s "an illusionary experience, such that consumers interact with personas (i.e., mediated representations of presenters, celebrities, or characters) as if they are present and engaged in a reciprocal relationship" (Labrecque 2014, 135). Simply put, PSI refers to the perception of a relationship or friendship with a media persona or organization (e.g., celebrities, athletes, talk shows hosts, etc.).

Over time, mediated interactions provide the media user with feelings of closeness or friendship with the persona (Labrecque 2014; Pegoraro 2014; Perse and Rubin 1989). As this "relationship" develops, the media user will seek out information and advice from the media persona as they would in an interpersonal relationship (Rubin, Perse, and Powell 1985). Despite the feelings of closeness and friendship that occur within PSI, the relationships are mostly one-sided (Frederick, Hambrick, and Clavio 2014). It is important to note that within PSI, it is the media persona that controls the degree of interaction with the media user (Frederick, Hambrick, and Clavio 2014). The media persona must break the "fourth wall" to reveal information about him or herself to the media user (Labrecque 2014, 136). This can be accomplished through strategic messaging using social media, specifically communicating with media users in a transparent manner that creates a sense of intimacy between the media persona and the user (Labrecque 2014).

PSI and Sports

PSI can be used as a lens to better understand fan-athlete interactions especially on social media (Kassing and Sanderson 2010). The celebrity status of athletes makes them frequent subjects of PSI (Kassing and Sanderson 2010; Pegoraro 2014). The emotional connection between fans and athletes can be classified as a parasocial relationship (Sun and Wu 2012). As with PSI relationships in other contexts, it is the job of the celebrity to choose to connect and engage with fans. In a sport context, "[t]he athlete must choose to take down that wall, effectively transforming the everyday fan from voyeur to digital acquaintance" (Frederick et al. 2012, 18).

Researchers have applied the PSI framework to examine the dynamic relationship between sport fans and sport entities (athletes, teams, and leagues) on social media. For example, Sanderson (2008a, 2008b) examined the interaction between fans and sport figures Mark Cuban and Curt Schilling (respectively) on their blogs. From the fan perspective, Kassing and Sanderson (2009) found that fans of Floyd Landis would provide him with career advice. In examining the athlete perspective, Kassing and Sanderson (2010) found that athletes participating in the Giro de Italia would share commentary and opinions providing fans with a behind the scenes look at what was going on during the race.

More recently, Frederick et al. (2014) used PSI as a theoretical framework to analyze relationships promoted by athletes using Twitter. Results of this study found that athletes were using the social networking site to promote both two-way and one-way (parasocial) relationships with fans. In other words, at some points the athletes used their account to interact with followers and at other times they used it primarily to broadcast information to followers. Frederick et al. (2012) surveyed Twitter users who followed athletes that were classified as either social or parasocial. Findings of this study found that users felt a "heightened sense of interpersonal closeness" with the athlete that exhibited a more social style of communication (Frederick et al. 2012, 481). This indicates that when the athlete appeared to be more social or interactive on Twitter, then the media user (i.e., fans) felt they knew the athlete better. Frederick et al. (2012) explain "because the social athlete appeared more social and approachable, many of his followers may have viewed him as someone they could have a relationship with and as someone who could actually fit within their everyday circle of friends" (495).

In an analysis of tweets from the National Hockey League (@nhl) during the 2012–2013 lockout, Frederick, Hambrick, and Clavio (2014) found that the @nhl used Twitter to promote identification and involvement among followers during the lockout. This was done by tweeting messages related to one of the four themes found in the analysis: "hope for the future, reminders of the past, information and reassurance, and media engagement" (Frederick et al. 2014, 25). Despite the lack of actual two-way communication in the @nhl tweets, the appearance of conversation as a mechanism for promoting PSI, which does not require two-way conversations between parties to occur (Frederick, Hambrick, and Clavio 2014).

TWITTER: CONNECTING FANS AND ATHLETES ONE TWEET AT A TIME

Social media has not only changed how fans and athletes interact (Pegoraro 2010); but it has also enhanced the overall experience of the sport fan (Kim and Song 2016). Prior to the social media age, any interaction between athletes and fans occurred in a carefully controlled environment usually coordinated by the team (Pegoraro 2010). But now, with the multitude of social media platforms available, there is potential for increased interaction between fans and athletes. For example, Twitter dramatically increases the odds that a fan will make contact with their favorite athlete (Frederick et al. 2012).

In one of the earliest studies of athletes on social media, Hambrick et al. (2010) found that the majority of athletes in the sample used Twitter to converse with followers. Of particular interest to note, those who had the largest following tended to exhibit higher levels of interactivity with followers, which indicates that fans respond positively to engagement efforts by professional athletes. Social media encounters between athletes and fans also carry increased significance for sport fans. For example, a retweet from an athlete on Twitter is considered to be the new form of autograph (Agyemang and Williams 2016; Williams et al. 2015). As such, a simple retweet or acknowledgement from an athlete has potential to further enhance identification between with fans, which benefits the athlete and team, by extension.

Related to social media strategy, athletes need to be authentic on social media in order to create a memorable experience for the fan (Pegoraro and Jinnah 2012). This authenticity includes publicly interacting with other athletes or the team on social media. For example, when athletes have public conversations with other athletes, fans are also part of these conversations, which creates a new dimension of the fan-athlete interaction (Hambrick et al. 2010). Through social media content fans are invited into the athlete's everyday life in a way that was previously unavailable. Fans also get a glimpse into the personal life and personality of the athlete.

THEMATIC ANALYSIS RESULTS

This chapter focuses on how sport teams can leverage the celebrity of athletes to enhance the fan-team relationship. As previously discussed, sport fans frequently have an emotional attachment to their favorite players that can transcend identification and loyalty to the team. As such, it is important for teams to create opportunities for fans to connect with and learn more about their favorite players. Previous studies have found that when fans have more access to the team, and especially players, then they are more likely to strengthen their identification with the team (Hambrick et al. 2010; Sutton et al. 1997). The goal, then, for sport brands should be to increase fan access to players (Meng, Stavros, and Westberg 2015; Sutton et al. 1997). This should provide additional incentives for fans to continue identification with the team (Hambrick et al. 2010; Thomson 2006). In other words, teams would benefit from athletes having a strong social media presence that includes personal information about the athlete, encourages fan interaction, and promotes the team. Findings of the analysis of tweets from professional sport teams revealed two strategies for incorporating athletes into the team's Twitter strategy: (1) athlete as team ambassador and (2) information about athletes.

Athletes as Team Ambassadors

The celebrity status of professional athletes can be used to increase awareness and attention to their team or sport (Williams et al. 2015). For example, professional basketball players in the 1990s (e.g., Michael Jordan, Larry Bird, and Magic Johnson) were able to generate increased attention and revenue for their teams, including increased ticket and merchandise sales (Hambrick and Mahoney 2011; Hausman and Leonard 1997). More recently, professional leagues, specifically the NBA, have emphasized individual star players when promoting games (Carlson and Donavan 2013). The value of the celebrity athlete is essential to maintaining high revenue streams provided by the selling of broadcast rights to games (Summers and Morgan 2008). Therefore, studying the role of athletes as celebrity brands can aid in understanding how athletes can provide additional value for their organization, whether it be an individual's team or sport (Agyemang and Williams 2016).

Results of the analysis revealed three ways that teams used players as ambassadors: (1) emphasizing the celebrity of athletes, (2) team promotional appearances, and (3) community appearances.

Emphasizing the Celebrity of Athletes

As previously discussed, the role of professional athletes as celebrity can be used to enhance not only identification with the athlete, but also with the team. Teams are responsible for creating content that encourage audience response and leveraging the celebrity of athletes is one way that teams can accomplish this (Culnan, McHugh, and Zubillaga 2010).

Several teams in the analysis highlighted the celebrity of athletes on the team. For example, the Atlanta Hawks tweeted about one of their players appearing at a concert: "@24Bazemore joined @chancetherapper on stage at his concert last week" (Atlanta Hawks[1]), this tweet was accompanied by a picture of Kent Bazemore at the concert. Still other teams emphasized the celebrity of athletes by featuring them with other celebrities. The Arizona Cardinals tweeted, "selfie from last year's #CardsCamp with @JordinSparks, @LarryFitzgerald, @MWest41, + @TysonChandler #NationalSelfieDay" (Arizona Cardinals[2]). These tweets demonstrate how teams can leverage the celebrity of athletes away from the field or court. Instances like these, behind the scene tours, and special treatment at concerts highlights the celebrity of athletes.

Team Promotional Appearances

Athletes often play a key role in facilitating fan identification with a team. In many cases, it is being a fan of a specific player that leads one to become a fan to the team. As such, sport brands should incorporate athletes into marketing efforts (Hopwood 2005). Furthermore, the lack of the presence of information about star players on mobile apps is a missed opportunity for teams to make a connection with fans (Watkins and Lewis 2014a). Teams need to be strategic about creating opportunities for fan-athlete engagement both online and offline.

Players frequently make appearances for team events where they can meet fans. Many of the teams in the sample used Twitter to promote such events. For example, the Dallas Stars tweeted, "Kari Lehtonen is signing autographs at @StarsHangar in @AACenter until 1:30 p.m. today! Get 40% off Stars gear in-store too!" (Dallas Stars[3]). This tweet was accompanied by a picture of fans with Lehtonen. Teams organize these events to bring fans closer to their favorite athletes. Promoting these tweets on social media increases the likelihood that fans will learn about and attend the event.

Community Appearances

Athletes were frequently featured in connection with local community events. Community appearances by athletes is closely connected to a team's corporate social responsibility efforts (CSR). CSR are activities that an organization takes on beyond its mission and serves the greater community. The high-profile nature of many sport and celebrity athletes lends itself to being a "force for good" in the world (Smith and Westerbeek, 2007, 49). The community-building component of sports and popularity of athletes can be used to bring awareness of relevant social issues affecting the local community (McGowan and Mahon 2009).

It is not surprising, then, that several teams featured athletes making community appearances related to the team's CSR efforts in their Twitter content. The Carolina Panthers tweeted about quarterback Cam Newton's celebrity kickball game for charity: "Cam [heart emoji] kickball. Find out why he uses it to help others" (Carolina Panthers[4]). This tweet was followed with a link to a five-minute video with Newton and highlights from the event. Other teams focused on player appearances at events with the local community. The Atlanta Hawks tweeted, "@foe23 surprised Jr. Hawks campers at Norcross High School" (Atlanta Hawks[5]), and similarly, the Dallas Mavericks tweeted, "Time to say goodbye! Thanks to @sdotcurry for visiting today's Hoop Camp presented by @Academy in Dallas! @MavsAcad" (Dallas Mavericks[6]). The Arizona Cardinals promoted an appearance from one of its former players for a local charity: "Join @kurt13warner, Brenda Warner, and Big Red this Saturday at UOPXStadium westvalleygivesaz.com The walk benefits @TreasureHouseAZ" (Arizona Cardinals[7]). By highlighting player participation in team CSR initiatives and community related activities, fans are able to see a different side of athletes and their commitment to the local community. These tweets provide insights to the values of professional athletes, which humanizes the athlete and makes these public figures more relatable. Additionally, player involvement in these initiatives furthers the team's CSR efforts, which can help enhance the relationship between the fan and the local community.

Providing Information about Athletes

Fans want to know more about the lives of their favorite athletes (Kassing and Sanderson 2010; Summers and Morgan 2008) and will seek out opportunities to learn more about and interact with their favorite athletes. Prior to social media entering the everyday lives of sport fans, "fans were kept at arm's length," which resulted in a widening of the gap between athletes and fans" (Pegoraro 2010, 503). Access to information about athletes provides another dimension to the celebrity athlete persona—one that exists on the court or field and one that exists beyond sports (Hambrick et al. 2010). Social media provides sport fans with information that might not be available through other forms of media. Taken together, these elements are useful for enhancing the relationship between fans and athletes, and subsequently, between the fan and the team. However, it is essential to note that information communicated on social media must be novel and authentic (Agyemang and Williams 2016). The goal should be to provide fans with new and interesting insights about the athlete that are as true and authentic as possible.

Results of the analysis revealed that teams provided insights and information about athletes through (1) features and profiles of athletes, (2) preparations for next season, (3) athlete awards and achievements, and (4) acknowledging player birthdays.

Features and Profiles of Athletes

Several teams provided information about players through the promotion of feature stories and profiles of players. The Arizona Cardinals tweeted a profile story about one of its players: "From working as a janitor @NFL Combine to working out at it. @Hogankri000's journey to the pros is remarkable" (Arizona Cardinals[8]). The feature tells the story of an undrafted rookie who worked through personal hardships to eventually be signed with an NFL team. Similarly, the Carolina Panthers tweeted a story about mild-manner and reserved cornerback James Bradberry: "You may THINK you know James Bradberry. Think again" (Carolina Panthers[9]). This feature highlights the personal attributes of athletes, which allows fans to get to know the player better as a person and athlete.

Player Preparation for Next Season

Other teams tweeted information about athletes preparing for the next season. The Atlanta Falcons tweeted, "Coming off an MVP season, #MattyIce wants Steve Sarkisian to find ways he can be even better. More" (Atlanta Falcons[10]). The Dallas Mavericks also highlighted how players were preparing for next season through a series of sponsored reports. One tweet read, "@DevHarris23 has been encouraged to see the young guys in the gym w/him this offseason" (Dallas Mavericks[11]). This tweet shows fans that the newer members of the team are taking their new position seriously and that the older, veteran players are excited about the prospects for the team. In another tweet, the Dallas Mavericks featured franchise player, Dirk Nowitzki: "After vacation time w/family, @swish41 is back in the gym preparing for a bounce-back season" (Dallas Mavericks[12]). Tweets like these show fans the commitment that athletes have to the team and to improving at their craft.

Player Awards and Achievements

Highlighting the awards and achievement of players is another strategy teams employed to emphasize athletes as elite. The above-average skills and athletic ability sets athletes apart from ordinary people. Teams celebrate this by highlighting player accomplishments on the field and throughout the season. During the season teams focused on player records and accomplishments, like the Houston Astros and Seattle Mariners did. The Astros tweeted, "Beltran's homer tonight as #431 for his career, tying Cal Ripken for 28th place on the all-time HR list" (Houston Astros[13]). Similarly, the Seattle Mariners tweeted, "With 22 so far, Mike Zunino has the Mariners record for RBI in a single season by a catcher. It's June 19th" (Mariners[14]). Another way that teams can honor players is by acknowledging their end-of-the season awards. For example, the Columbus BlueJackets recognized team captain Nick Foligno's winning of the King Clancy Memorial trophy (ColumbusBlueJackets[15]). Similarly, the Dallas Mavericks and Atlanta Hawks each acknowledged honors received by two of their players being selected by the NBA Players Association as captains for the 2017 NBA Africa Game (Atlanta Hawks,[16] Dallas Mavericks[17]). These tweets recognize the individual achievements of athletes and also generate excitement for what the players can continue to do.

Player Birthdays

An interesting theme to emerge from the analysis was wishing players a happy birthday from the team account. These tweets included simple birthday messages, opportunities for fan engagement, and additional information about the player. For example, the LA Kings tweeted a simple happy birthday to one of its athletes: "Wishing Jonny Brodzinski the best birthday today" (#LAKings[18]), which included a graphic featuring Brodzinski. While the Dallas Mavericks used a birthday as an opportunity to engage fans: "We all know what day it is!! Join us in wishing @swish41 a very special Happy Birthday! What's your favorite Dirk memory?! #MavsBirthdays" (Dallas Mavericks[19]). The Atlanta Falcons also solicited fan engagement with a birthday announcement: "RT [retweet] to wish former Falcons WR [wide receiver] @TerranceMathis a Happy Birthday! He ranks no. 2 in franchise history in receiving touchdowns" (Atlanta Falcons[20]). Promoting player birthdays on Twitter is another way the team can help bridge the distance between fans and athletes.

CONCLUSION

This chapter examined how teams leverage the celebrity of professional athletes. Previous studies have found that athletes are often the tie that connects fans to teams (Agyemang and Williams 2016; Carlson and Donavan 2013). Fans will gravitate to and identify with a team because of the players on the team. Identification with an athlete has a significant influence on fan consumption behaviors including watching games and spending money on team-related merchandise (Carlson and Donavan 2013). Furthermore, emotional attachment is important for the development of lasting fan-team relationships (Thomson 2006). In a sport context, the emotional attachment between a fan and an athlete is essential for developing a relationship with the team. Therefore, it is important to better understand how athletes can be used to enhance the relationship between the team and the fan. The chapter drew on parasocial interaction as a theoretical framework for better understanding how relationships develop between the public and media personalities.

The emergence of social networking sites, like Twitter, has provided fans with unprecedented information about teams and athletes. Information is the currency of social media, and sport fans are avid users of social media to find information about their favorite teams and athletes. Through social media, fans learn about their favorite players both on and off the field. Additionally, the interactive nature of social media increases the likelihood that a fan will interact with an athlete, which has created a new "integrated media experience for fans" (Kassing and Sanderson 2010, 248). The possibility for interaction adds a new dimension to the fan experience. Through social media actual rather than imaginary interaction can take place between athletes and fans (Pegoraro 2010). Social media represents the *potential* for a more balanced relationship between the media persona and the media user (Stever and Lawson 2013, emphasis added). As such, teams should implement strategies that enhance identification between fans and athletes (Carlson and Donavan 2013). Taken together, these two factors have potential to enhance the feelings of connection fans have with professional athletes and ultimately the fan-team relationship (Hambrick et al. 2010).

In order to better understand how social media can be used to enhance PSI with a media figure, more focus should go to the content of the social media messages (Labrecque 2014). Messages produced for social media should provide insights to the athlete's life and career (Kassing and Sanderson 2010). Additionally, for professional sports teams, where athletes are celebrities and brands in their own right, getting the players involved with the social media strategy is one way that sports teams can encourage fans to interact with the sports organization.

In the analysis reported in this chapter, results revealed two key themes in tweets involving athletes—the players as team ambassadors and providing information about athletes. Having players take on an ambassador role for the team is important for bringing increased attention to the team. Based on the findings, teams did this by emphasizing the celebrity of athletes, including information about team promotional events, and promoting player involvement in the community. In terms of providing information about players, tweets fell in one of the following categories: features and profile stories, player preparations for the new season, awards and achievement, and birthdays.

This analysis focused primarily on the original content created by teams (not retweets) to promote the fan-athlete relationship. However, there are other ways that teams can facilitate the connection between fans and athletes. One suggestion is to produce content that takes on a more conversational tone that includes cues that gives the media user the illusion they are listening and interacting with users (Labrecque 2014; Stever and Lawson 2013). From a team perspective, incorporating content from the athlete's social media account can provide fans with additional information about their favorite players (Meng, Stavros, and Westberg 2015). Athletes (and teams) can create social media content that enhances parasocial interaction by including components that indicates they are listening to fans (Labrecque 2014). Furthermore, marketers should encourage athletes to retweet or share team-related social media content to followers (Agyemang and Williams 2016). These are just a few suggestions, but more research is needed to better understand the dynamics of fan-athlete interactions on social media (Clavio and Kian 2010).

NOTES

1. Atlanta Hawks [ATLHawks]. (2017, June 19). @24Bazemore joined @chancetherapper on stage at his concert last week! (via @RobbCohen1) [Tweet]. Retrieved from https://twitter.com/ATLHawks/status/876933364191834112/photo/1

2. Arizona Cardinals [AZCardinals]. (2017, June 21). Selfie from last year's #CardsCamp with @JordinSparks, @LarryFitzgerald, @mwest41 + @TysonChandler. #NationalSelfieDay [Tweet]. Retrieved from https://twitter.com/i/web/status/877556763972648960

3. Kari Lehtonen is signing autographs at @StarsHangar in @AACenter until 1:30 PM today! Get 40% off Stars gear in-store too! [Tweet]. Retrieved from https://twitter.com/i/web/status/871043815695466496

4. Carolina Panthers [Panthers]. (2017, June 10). Cam [heart emoji] kickball. Find out why he uses it to help others. Panth.rs/8VaGD1 [Tweet]. Retrieved from https://twitter.com/Panthers/status/873636890771107840/photo/1

5. Atlanta Hawks [ATLHawks]. (2017, June 14). @foe23 surprised Jr. Hawks campers at Norcross High School [Tweet]. Retrieved from https://twitter.com/ATLHawks/status/875012602040135685/photo/1

6. Dallas Mavericks [dallasmavs]. (2017, June 21). Time to say goodbye! Thanks to @sdotcurry for visiting today's Hoop Camp presented by @Academy in Dallas! @MavsAcad [Tweet]. Retrieved from https://twitter.com/dallasmavs/status/877618591499042817/video/1

7. Arizona Cardinals [AZCardinals]. (2017, June 21). Join @kurt13warner, Brenda Warner, and & Big Red this Saturday at @UOPXStadium westvalleygivesaz.com The walk benefits @TreasureHouseAZ [Tweet]. Retrieved from https://twitter.com/i/web/status/877552583568535553

8. Arizona Cardinals [AZCardinals]. (2017, June 21). From working as a janitor @NFL Combine to working out at it. @hogankri000's journey to the pros is remarkable. [Tweet]. Retrieved from https://twitter.com/AZCardinals/status/877662233492312066

9. Carolina Panthers [Panthers]. (2017, June 14). You may THINK you know James Bradberry Think again panth.rs/1vscpO [Tweet]. Retrieved from https://twitter.com/Panthers/status/875123430437376000/photo/1

10. Atlanta Falcons [AtlantaFalcons]. (2017, June 8). Coming off an MVP season, #MayyIce wants Steve Sarkisian to find ways he can be even better. MORE atlfal.co.nz/2s8UP7s [Tweet]. Retrieved from https://twitter.com/i/web/status/872983803484090368

11. Dallas Mavericks [dallasmavs]. (2017, June 21).@Dev34Harris has been encouraged to see the young guys in the gym w/him this offseason. @BBVACompass Report: go.mavs.com/I5BH [Tweet]. Retrieved from https://twitter.com/i/web/status/877640607115563008

12. Dallas Mavericks [dallasmavs]. (2017, June 12). After vacation time w/family, @swish41 is back in the gym preparing for a bounce-back season. @BBVACompass REPORT: go.mavs.com/I5yH [Tweet]. Retrieved from https://twitter.com/i/web/status/874368403502383104

13. Houson Astros [astros]. (2917, June 21). Beltran's homer tonight was #431 for his career, tying Cal Ripken for 48th place on the all-time HR list! [Tweet]. Retrieved from https://twitter.com/astros/status/877408694903898112/video/1

14. Mariners [Mariners]. (2017, June 19). With 22 so far, Mike Zunino has the Mariners record for RBI in a single month by a catcher. It is June 19th. [Tweet]. Retrieved from https://twitter.com/Mariners/status/876892599600074752/photo/1

15. ColumbusBlueJackets [BlueJacketsNHL]. (2017, June 20). CONGRATS to #CBJ captain @NickFoligno on winning the King Clancy Memorial Trophy!!! [Tweet]. Retrieved from https://twitter.com/BlueJacketsNHL/status/877303891074756609/photo/1

16. Atlanta Hawks [ATLHawks]. (2017, June 19). @ThaboSefolosha on being named captain for the 2017 @NBA Africa Game [Tweet]. Retrieved from https://twitter.com/ATLHawks/status/876827446145888260/photo/1

17. Dallas Mavericks [dallasmavs]. (2017, June 19). Dirk Nowitzki will captain Team World in NBA Africa Game 2017! Go.mavs.com/I/5zY [Tweet]. Retrieved from https://twitter.com/dallasmavs/status/876815399475568641/photo/1

18. #LAKings [LAKings]. (2017, June 19). Wishing Jonny Brodzinski the best birthday today! [Tweet]. Retrieved from https://twitter.com/LAKings/status/876877302319034368/photo/1

19. Dallas Mavericks [dallasmavs]. (2017, June 19). We all know what day it is!!! Join us in wishing @swish41 a very special Happy Birthday! What's your favorite Dirk memory?! #MavsBirthdays [Tweet]. Retrieved from https://twitter.com/i/web/status/876794279355613184

20. Atlanta Falcons [AtlantaFalcons]. (2017, June 7). RT to wish former Falcons WR @TerranceMathis a Happy Birthday! He ranks No. 2 in franchise history in receiving touchdowns. [Tweet]. Retrieved from https://twitter.com/i/web/status/872446814175113216

Chapter 6

Dialogue

Sport brands have been on the forefront of creating unique online engage-ment opportunities for fans. One strategy sport brands frequently use to engage fans on social media is to develop branded hashtags that fans are encouraged to incorporate into their online posts. For example, the NBA's Toronto Raptors frequently use the hashtag #WeTheNorth as a nod to being the only Canadian team in the league, and the NFL's Carolina Panthers use the hashtag #KeepPounding, which has become a rallying cry for the team. In 2016, Twitter unveiled a new addition to the hashtag called the "hashflag" (Newport 2017; Schwartz 2016) for NBA and NFL teams. When a Twitter user posts a tweet with a team-designated hashtag, an emoji related to the team accompanies the tweet.

The enhanced communication capabilities afforded by Web 2.0 technolo-gies have resulted in consumer-brand communications that are capable of being more immediate and interactive (Brodie et al. 2011). Scholars have since studied various social media strategies and platforms that organizations can use to create an interactive experience for fans. In particular, the concept of dialogue is frequently used as a lens to examine relationship-building strategies employed by organizations using social media. Dialogue is a strategy that "helps an organization manage the organization-public rela-tionship by providing publics with the opportunity to ask questions, express viewpoints, and better understand organizational processes" (Bruning, Dials, and Shirka 2008, 241).

This chapter examines the role of dialogue in relationship building. The following sections discuss the importance of dialogue for relationship building as well as reviews the existing research on dialogue and social media. The dialogic principles, a set of five principles frequently used to assess online relationship building, are discussed. This chapter reports findings of a thematic analysis of Twitter content and, by looking at the specific content of the message, identifies relationship-building strategies.

LET'S TALK: DIALOGUE FOR RELATIONSHIP BUILDING

In order to understand the use of dialogue as a relationship-building tool, it is important to understand the origins of the concept. Martin Buber is widely considered to be the first to define the modern concept of dialogue. According to Buber's conceptualization, dialogue "involves an effort to recognize the value of the other" and his work is based on the concepts of "reciprocity, mutuality, involvement, and openness" (as cited in Kent and Taylor 2002, 22). Dialogic communication is "any negotiated exchange of ideas and opinions" (Kent and Taylor 1998, 325) and dialogue is "about the process of open and negotiated discussion" (Kent and Taylor 1998, 325). There are five tenets of dialogue: (1) mutuality, or the idea that organizations and publics are linked together; (2) propinquity, if the public is willing to voice their opinion then the organization should listen; (3) empathy, a spirit of trust should exist between both parties; (4) risk, or the acceptance that some control is lost in the communication exchange; and (5) commitment, where both parties are committed to the relationship (Kent and Taylor 2002).

Based on their conceptualization of dialogue, Kent and Taylor (1998) proposed five principles for engaging in dialogue online: (1) the dialogic loop, (2) usefulness of information, (3) generation of return visits, (4) the rule of conversation of visitors, and (5) intuitiveness/ease of interface. Initially these principles were conceptualized for application to websites, but as new social media platforms emerged, the principles were adapted to fit various social media platforms.

Usefulness of Information

The usefulness of information principle suggests that content disseminated online should be relatively useful for all publics (Kent and Taylor 1998). In essence, the public, or in this case sport fans, should find the information they consume online to be useful and beneficial. The idea behind this principle is that if the user finds the content as useful, then they are more likely to continue to follow the organization online or on social media where fans have a plethora of options for information.

Dialogic Loop

Of all the principles, the dialogic loop best exemplifies the use of two-way communication for relationship building. This principle proposes that organizations should go beyond disseminating information using the one-way, broadcast model by incorporating a mutual negotiation with publics (Kent and Taylor 1998). Most social media platforms allow for a dialogic loop through the integration of a comments feature. For example, Facebook users can leave a comment on an organization's post or a Twitter user can use the "@" mention feature to directly reply to tweets.

Conservation of Visitors

The rule of conservation of visitors principle suggests organizations should keep the user engaged in its online space (Kent and Taylor 1998). The under-lying assumption to this principle is that once a user leaves the organization's online space, then they may not return. This principle has been operationalized in research studies as integrating the social media presence of the organization. For example, using Twitter to drive users to the organization's Instagram feed, or using Facebook to link to the organization's blog to increase blog traffic.

Generation of Return Visits

The generation of return visits principle implies that it is the job of the organization to create content that will keep users visiting the organization's social media feed. Organizations can do this by maintaining an active online presence and frequently updating the social media account (Kent and Taylor 1998). Just having an online presence is not enough to keep users interested; instead, there should be consistent content readily available for users. As researchers applied this principle into social media, this definition evolved to include interactive elements of social media including multimedia components such as embedded pictures and videos.

Intuitiveness/Ease of Interface

The last principle, intuitiveness/ease of interface, is more relevant to the appli-cation of these principles to websites rather than social media. Organizations should create a website that has a clean interface and is easy to navigate and contains information (Kent and Taylor 1998). As these principles have been applied more to social media, this principle is frequently omitted from research because the interface is the same for all users.

These five principles have guided much of the research related to dialogue and online relationship building. The following section provides an overview of the existing body of research on dialogue and social media.

RESEARCH ON DIALOGUE AND SOCIAL MEDIA

As social media is integrated into more strategic communication initiatives, researchers have worked to examine these new communication channels to determine how it can be used to build, enhance, and maintain relationships between organizations and consumers. The primary theoretical perspective guiding this research is the dialogic principles that were described in the previous section. Among the first online relationship-building tools studied were organizational websites. Findings of research by Taylor and Kent (2004), Gordon and Berhow (2009), and Ingenhoff and Koelling (2009) suggested the dialogic capabilities of websites were not fully utilized. While Park and Reber (2008) found that dialogic activity on websites could promote control mutuality, trust, satisfaction, openness, and intimacy. Seltzer and Mitrook (2007) added that blogs were actually more effective than websites at promoting dialogic principles.

As social media platforms, such as Facebook and Twitter, were incorporated into integrated marketing communication strategies, researchers turned their attention to how dialogue was integrated into specific social media strategies. Bortree and Seltzer (2009) studied the dialogic strategies of environmental advocacy groups on Facebook. They found that among the groups in their study, most of these organizations were not engaging their publics in dialogue using Facebook. Waters et al. (2009) found that nonprofit organizations were not using all of the Facebook applications available to them. However, Waters et al. (2011) found that university health centers with a large following on Facebook were more likely to employ dialogic principles on their page. Sweetser and Lariscy's (2008) study of Facebook comments during midterm elections found that people who wrote on a candidate's wall considered themselves to be "friendly" with the candidate, even though they rarely responded.

Specific to Twitter, Rybalko and Seltzer (2010) found that among Fortune 500 companies, organizations with a dialogic orientation were more likely to employ the conservation of visitors principle. Lovejoy, Waters, and Saxton (2012) found that among nonprofit organizations Twitter was used primarily to distribute one-way messages to audiences. Similarly, Linvill, McGee, and Hicks (2012) found that colleges and universities primarily use Twitter as an outlet for disseminating messages. Waters and Williams (2011) noted that information sharing was the primary focus of social media use among public relations practitioners.

Dialogue, Sports, and Social Media

Specific to sports, there are few studies examining how sports organizations use dialogue to build relationships with fans online. In one of the earliest studies, the Twitter accounts of twenty-two professional athletes (eleven male and eleven female) was analyzed to determine whether they employed the dialogic principles (Watkins & Lewis 2014b). Results indicated that athletes tended to employ the generation of return visits principle the most, followed by usefulness of information. Based on these findings, it can be determined that professional athletes tended to produce content that can be categorized as one-way communication but was designed to keep fans returning to their Twitter feed and can be mostly considered one-way communication.

Based on the findings of the previous study, a follow-up study was conducted to examine the audience perception of dialogic activity on social media (Watkins 2016). The goal of this study was to determine how receptive sport fans were to dialogic activity on social media. Results of a survey indicated that sports fans were more interested in following professional athletes for information and entertainment purposes, both of which are largely manifest through one-way communication tactics. Consequently, respondents also reported they were more likely to consume social media content rather than engage with the athlete. According to these results, sports fans did not seem to be interested in engaging in direct dialogue with professional athletes.

A third study using experimental design to determine the effectiveness of the dialogic principles for relationship building between athletes and fans (Watkins 2017). Findings of this study revealed that fans were more responsive to tweets that employed the usefulness of information principle. The audience indicated they would be more likely to engage with the athlete when they found information in the tweet to be useful. From this study, it can be concluded that in some instances one-way communication between athletes and fans could be more beneficial to relationship building than two-way communication, which had long been the assumption.

The common thread throughout research on the dialogic principles and social media is the focus on whether or not the dialogic principles were present in social media content. Most of the existing research on the dialogic principles approach them as a checklist for achieving dialogue; however, Taylor and Kent (2014) disagree with this line of thinking. They argue, "the biggest flaw in how dialogue has been examined in web-based public relations has involved treating the features of dialogue as a series of categories that had to be present for the potential for dialogue" (Taylor and Kent 2014, 388). Successful dialogue is not necessarily about the process, or how mutual understanding is achieved, but should be measured by outcomes (Kent and Taylor 2002). This chapter investigates the use of dialogue as a relationship-building strategy, the outcome of interest, therefore, is the relationship between the fans and the team.

To get to the outcome, an under-researched aspect of dialogue, is to examine the content of the messages. To that end, this study examines the messages communicated by teams to fans using Twitter. Using the dialogic principles as a guiding theoretical framework, tweets were analyzed to determine messaging strategies that promote mutual understanding. Since the unit of analysis was individual tweets, the ease of interface principle was excluded since all Twitter accounts look the same.

THEMATIC ANALYSIS RESULTS

Usefulness of Information

Sport brands tend to tweet a lot, and the topics covered varies depending on what the team is doing and time of year (e.g., draft, offseason, pre-season, etc.). Tweets from the study were analyzed in terms of what teams were tweeting about that could be considered useful for sport fans. Two broad categories emerged from the analysis—(1) team building news and (2) team performance.

Team Building News

Tweets related to team building news focused on providing fans with information about efforts to build the team's roster. These tweets included (1) news about players and (2) information about upcoming drafts, trades, and player signings.

Player News

Tweets that included news about players ranged from providing information about players recovering from injury, retirement ceremonies, and statistics about current players. Keeping up with injury and recovery status is important for fans to know what is going on with the team and their favorite players. Seeing a player recover from injury and ready to rejoin the team can excite a fan base for what is to come. For example, the Carolina Panthers tweeted a story about Michael Oher rejoining the team after going through concussion protocol: "Michael Oher is back in Charlotte after reconnecting with the #Panthers More Info" (Carolina Panthers[1]). Teams also used Twitter to update fans on the decisions current players were making about their future, for example the Arizona Cardinals tweeted: "Larry Fitzgerald discusses when he will address his future" (Arizona Cardinals[2]).

Teams that were in-season during the time of data collection (the MLB) kept fans up-to-date with player stats. For example, the San Francisco Giants tweeted, "Buster Posey continues to pace NL catchers in All-Star balloting. Help keep him on top: sfgiants.com/vote #BustTheVote #SFGiants" (San Francisco Giants[3]) and "ICYMI: Austin Slater recorded a career-best four hits last night and now has 12 hits in his last five games" #SFGiants" (San Francisco Giants[4]).

Draft, Trade, and Signings News

A major theme related to useful information was tweets that included direct team-building news such as draft information and news about trades and/or player signings. During the time of data analysis, several of the team were involved in the draft. The NHL was having an expansion draft for a new team, and teams used Twitter to keep fans up-to-date on the implications of the expansion draft for their team (#LAKings,[5] Columbus Blue Jackets,[6] Dallas Stars[7]). Related to this, the Dallas Stars tweeted a four-minute video that provided fans with information about why certain decisions were made regarding the expansion draft: "Our protected list is out, and @OwnenNewkirk provides some insight on why certain players were protected and others were not" (Dallas Stars[8]). The Seattle Mariners gave fans an inside look at the Mariners Draft Room so fans could catch a glimpse of the decision-making process in action (Mariners[9]). Teams across leagues all tweeted information related to signings (#LAKings,[10] AZCardinals,[11] Atlanta Falcons[12]), while other teams provided fans with insights into the team's roster building plans. For example, the Dallas Mavericks tweeted, "Mavericks may look at upgrading at the point guard position with their top 10 draft pick @BBVACompass REPORT" (Dallas Mavericks[13]). Similarly, many teams used Twitter to introduce fans to their new signees (Mariners,[14] LAKings,[15] Atlanta Hawks,[16] and Carolina Panthers[17]).

Tweets across all of these categories provide information that is useful to fans. Prior to social media entering the sports world, teams relied on traditional media to get information to fan, but unless the news was about a marquee player or team, the coverage would not have the same level of depth that teams can provide fans with through Twitter. Many of the tweets in the analysis were accompanied by graphics, videos, or links to full stories where fans can get different perspectives about the status of the team.

Team Performance

In addition to team building information, tweets also contained information about the team's performance. Given that during the time of data collection and analysis, most of the teams were in the off-season, many of these tweets were related to either a recap of the previous season or a preview of the upcoming season. For example, the Golden State Warriors tweeted, "A look back on one of the more impressive & entertaining seasons in NBA history" (GoldenStateWarriors[18]). The Atlanta Falcons tweeted scouting reports on the teams they were scheduled to face in the next season, drawing on the previous season for context. For example: "We split our series against the Bucs last year. What weapons has Tampa Bay added since then? Scouting Report" (Atlanta Falcons[19]).

During data analysis, the NFL teams were finishing off-season training camps, and teams used this as an opportunity to update fans on the status of the team. For example, the Arizona Cardinals tweeted, "@Cardschatter's nine takeways from the offseason program" (Arizona Cardinals[20]). And the Atlanta Falcons gave fans an inside look at practice, with a link to a thirty-second video of a coach wearing a microphone during practice (Atlanta Falcons[21]). Other teams, like Atlanta Hawks, gave fans a glimpse of pre-draft workouts (Atlanta Hawks[22]). In addition to roster building, this kind of specialized content puts fans in the middle of the team and keeps them up-to-date on not only who will be playing but also how preparations for next season are going.

As previously discussed, much of the previous research has centered on the assumption that the two-way communication capabilities of social media are the driving force for online relationship building. However, researchers are finding that the one-way messages distributed via social media should not be overlooked as significant relationship-building strategies. McAllister-Spooner and Kent (2009) found that useful information and the dialogic loop are significant predictors of responsiveness to organizational communication efforts. Similarly, Watkins (2017) found that among four of the dialogic principles, tweets utilizing the usefulness of information principle were more likely to have a significant influence on relationship-building activities such as engagement and attitude. Teams should be tuned in to the information needs of fans and integrate this content into social media strategies.

Conservation of Visitors and Generation of Return Visits

Given the similarities between the defining characteristics of conservation of visitors and generation of return visits of these principles, this analysis looked at features that exemplified these principles in tandem. More specifically, the analysis identified tweets that integrated social media content and demonstrated the multimedia capabilities of Twitter. Taken together, these features function to keep fans involved and returning to the team's Twitter feed.

Social Media Integration

Social media managers have a variety of social media platforms to choose from when developing their social media strategy. The use of multiple platforms provides organizations with the opportunity to integrate its social media strategy and keep users engaged across platforms. Integrating social media platforms allows brands to tell a consistent brand story that reinforces the brand identity of the organization (Rybalko and Seltzer 2010). Throughout the dataset, teams would send tweets encouraging users to check out something on another social media profile. The Dallas Mavericks tweeted, "Tune in to FB [Facebook] live during the 2 o'clock hour to watch our very own @MavsChamp rappel down @ReunionTower" (Dallas Mavericks[23]), and the Arizona Cardinals encouraged fans to tune into Periscope for a live question and answer session with the team's president (Arizona Cardinals[24]). Teams also used Twitter to encourage fans to check out the team's podcasts (#LAKings,[25] Dallas Mavericks,[26] Mariners[27]) and mobile app (#LAKings[28]).

Multimedia Features

Most social media platforms allow multimedia content, which include pictures, graphics, gifs, and videos that are incorporated into social media content. There has since been a steady increase in the sharing of photos and videos on social media sites (Khang, Ki, and Lee 2012).

The ability to include high quality visual content on social media provides not only a way for organizations to create more interesting content, but it also allows the organization to reinforce its brand identity (Watkins and Lee 2016). By continually exposing fans to visual imagery related to the team (through multimedia content on social media) sports organizations can reinforce their brand image and organizational identity (Lee et al. 2008; Magrath and McCormick 2013; McNely 2012).

Twitter allows users to embed multimedia content into their Twitter feed. Nearly every team in the analysis incorporated a variety of multimedia elements into its Twitter content. The Carolina Panthers used the video capabilities to create a video series called "Captain's Corner" where Captain Munnerlynn would conduct man on the street interviews with the people of Charlotte: "We'll make your Monday morning more fun! Tune into the debut of Captain's Corner, starring @captain_41!" (Carolina Panthers[29]). The Dallas Mavericks provided fans with audio of an interview with a player (Dallas Mavericks[30]). And the Seattle Mariners provided fans with a weekly recap of game highlights specifically for Twitter: "you know Ben Gamel's wild catch made the cut. What else is in the #DidYouSeaThat Plays of the Week? Just watch" (Mariners[31]).

The multimedia capabilities of Twitter allow teams to provide fans with a closer look at the game. Teams featured in-game videos of players wearing microphones, which gives fans an even closer look at what goes on during the game. The Columbus Blue Jackets did this by tweeting a teaser of what the players said during the game: "I almost got decapitated! The best moments from #CBJ mic'd up this season" (ColumbusBlueJackets[32]). The San Francisco Giants posted a tweet with a video of a player at bat from multiple angles: "A fresh look at @BusterPosey's rally-starting double in the 7th #SFGiants #BustTheVote" (San Francisco Giants[33]).

Social media users tend to respond more favorably to visual images and multimedia content (McNely 2012). Sport fans, in particular, seem to gravitate toward the video content available on social media, which allows them to catch replays of their favorite team. For example, in a survey college sports fans found users were more likely to watch videos online, and these findings suggest "a desire on the audience's part for sensory-rich media" (Clavio and Walsh 2014, 15). By providing this kind of all access multimedia content, teams are giving fans access to information and entertainment not previously available, which keep them coming back and engaging in their online spaces.

Dialogic Loop

As previously discussed, the actual use of two-way communication on social media, using the traditional operationalization of dialogue, has been minimal (Levenshus 2010; Waters and Williams 2011; Watkins 2016). Even though scholars and practitioners alike have lauded social media for its role in facilitating two-way communication, there is limited evidence to support that this is actually occurring (Waters and Williams 2011). Instead, alternative conceptualizations of dialogue, specific to social media, are necessary (Watkins 2017). As such, the tweets in this study were analyzed to determine what strategies teams use to encourage interaction beyond direct two-way communication. Results of the analysis revealed two strategies for encouraging interaction with fans: (1) branded hashtags and (2) encouraging user-generated content.

Branded Hashtags

Twitter hashtags are a feature of Twitter that function to annotate tweets and connect users with broader topics and conversations happening on Twitter (Feng and Wang 2014). Hashtags are words or a group of words that follow a hashtag sign (#) on Twitter and provides a way to identify relevant topics for the tweet (Smith and Smith 2012; Feng and Wang 2014). Through the use of hashtags, users can determine what topics are popular (or trending) on

Twitter (Smith and Smith 2012). Hashtags also help to increase the visibility of tweets (Page 2012). Hashtags function as a way to "broadcast in one-to-many updates, which emphasize the declarative forms or imperatives that in turn seek to persuade the addressed audience to engage with the promoted commodity" (Page 2012, 198). In other words, using a hashtag to identify a tweet encourages fans to incorporate that hashtag into their tweets about the game. As a result, the community building function of Twitter is realized.

Nearly every team in the analysis created a branded hashtag, but the actual use of the hashtags was not always consistent in the Twitter data. Some teams had several branded hashtags to represent different aspects of the team (see Dallas Mavericks and Arizona Cardinals), while other teams limited the number of branded hashtags used (see Atlanta Hawks). It is also interesting to note that several teams in the analysis created branded hashtags around certain players. Team-specific branded hashtags can be found in table 6.1.

Specifically, for sport fans, Twitter users can use the team hashtag as an outlet for identifying with the team, or "a virtual wearing of team jersey" (Smith and Smith 2012, 551). When fans include a hashtag in their tweets, they are proclaiming their identification with the group, which is a public aspect of social identification. From the sports organization perspective, the organization itself can create hashtags to identify their team and tweet information about specific games. In fact, Twitter users were more likely to adopt the hashtags that they see in the moment (Smith and Smith 2012). A proactive sports organization can create and promote their own hashtags related to their team and allow fans to incorporate those hashtags into their tweets.

Encourage User-Generated Content

While traditional conceptualizations of dialogue may not be suited for social media, it is worth examining the features of social media to determine how other forms of interaction between a brand and audience, or sport team and fan, can occur. Social media enables consumers to take on a more active role in the relationship by sharing their experiences with a brand through user-generated content (UGC). UGC includes the brand-related content created by the consumer (Malthouse et al. 2016). In order to be classified as user-generated content, three criteria must be met: (1) the content must be available to the public over the Internet, (2) the content must reflect a certain amount of creative effort, and (3) must be created outside the professional routines and practices (Christodoulides, Jevons, and Bonhomme 2012, 2).

Several teams in the analysis encouraged users to get engaged by creating UGC. The Atlanta Hawks used online quizzes to engage followers: "Can you name all of our first-round draft picks since 2000? Try here" (Atlanta Hawks[34]). This tweet included a link to an online quiz. When it was announced

Table 6.1. Branded Hashtags

Team	Total Branded Hashtags	Hashtags
LA Kings	2	#FitToBeKing; #LAKings
Houston Astros	7	#Astros; #AstrosWin; #SpringerDingers; #AstrosAfterDark; #AstrosMoments; #JakeDay; #EarnIt
Arizona Cardinals	7	#AllAZ; #BirdGang; #BeRedSeeRed; #MathieuMondays; #P2Tuesdays; #FitzFridays; #AZCardinals
Atlanta Falcons	7	#RiseUp; #InBrotherhood; #EatFree; #Agent12; #MattyIce; #JetJones; #TurboTaylor
Atlanta Hawks	1	#TrueToAtlanta
Carolina Panthers	4	#Panthers; #KeepPounding; #PlayLikeAPanther; #OneCarolina
Columbus BlueJackets	1	#CBJ
Dallas Mavericks	8	#MFFL/MFFLS; #dallasmavs; #Mavericks; #MavsUpgrade; #MavsDraft17; #MavsSpiked17; #MavsBirthdays; #MFFLStories
Dallas Stars	2	#GoStars; #Stars
Golden State Warriors	5	#DubNation; #StrengthInNumbers; #WarriorsParade; #SPLASH; #Warriors Ground
Seattle Mariners	2	#GoMariners; #DidYouSeaThat
San Francisco Giants	2	#SFGiants; #WeAreSF

that the Olympics would include 3-on-3 basketball, the Hawks also tweeted, "What 3 all-time Hawks would you have on your 3-on-3 Olympic team?" (AtlantaHawks[35]). These tweets are effective because it gets fans thinking and debating about who are the best Hawks players of all time while encouraging fans to share their answers on Twitter.

The LA Kings were also prolific in encouraging user-generated content. One tweet encouraged fans to create content for the team app: "Show us how you celebrated your dad today by posting in the 'My Hockey Dad' capsule on the LA Kings Fan App!" (#LAKings[36]). Another promotion encouraged fans to get active by beating the team's mascot in a squats contest: Beat Bailey's 23 squats and post your video with #FitToBeKing to win @24hourfitness and Lenny & Larry's prizes" (#LAKings[37]).

Teams also provided incentives for fans to get involved. For example, the Houston Astros encouraged fans to vote for their players for the All-Star Game by offering a #VoteAstros t-shirt: "Another day, another chance to win a #VoteAstros t-shirt! Reply to this tweet with your ballot for a chance to win" (Houston Astros[38]). For Father's Day, the Astros gave away a Father's Day Prize Pack for fans who submitted pictures of Astros fans with their fathers (Houston Astros[39]). These are just a few examples of the creative strategies teams employed on Twitter to encourage fans to create content relevant to the team.

Creating opportunities for UGC is of particular interest to strategic communicators (Malthouse et al. 2016). Research has found that the creation of UGC could increase customer-based brand equity, and the relationship between UGC and brand equity is symbiotic (Christodoulides, Jevons, and Bonhomme 2012). They also found that consumers are more likely to engage with a brand that has a high equity, and the equity of a brand increases as more consumers engage with the brand. Engagement and UGC can be used as a method for determining the effectiveness of social media marketing programs (Schiviniski, Christodoulides, and Dabrowski 2016).

CONCLUSION

Relationship formation is a process of adaptation and response (Broom, Casey, and Ritchey 1997), and dialogue is essential for relationship building (Kent and Taylor 1998). Organizations with a dialogic orientation in social media content, or an engaging and interactive strategy, can enhance its relationship-building efforts (Bruning, Dials, and Shirka 2008). Similarly, those with a higher the level of interaction on Twitter, the higher the audience will perceive the quality of the organization/public relationship (Saffer,

Sommerfeldt and Taylor 2013). As such, the concept of dialogue is an important consideration when investigating organization-public relationships.

When organizations fully cooperate in the communication process, then the relationship with the public is more realized. However, it is important to note that in the social media context, cooperation in the communication process may not necessarily mean direct two-way communication. Waters and Williams (2011) support this sentiment, suggesting "there are times in organizational communication campaigns when one-way messages are preferred and more helpful than taking a symmetrical approach; there are others when conversation and negotiation will yield the most gain for the organization" (359–60)." Beyond that, the nature of social media (e.g., the massive number of users and the speed at which information is updated) means that it is not always feasible for an organization, especially a sport brand with millions of followers, to have the resources to respond directly to all followers. It is important that researchers and practitioners reconsider what is meant by dialogue on social media.

Much of the research on social media and relationship building have examined content for the presence of the dialogic principles. While this research has yielded interesting findings about organizational approaches to social media, it often overstates the importance of two-way communication. In this chapter, the content of Twitter activity from sport brands was analyzed to determine what messages teams were communicating with fans using the dialogic principles as a guiding theoretical framework.

Related to the usefulness of information principle, teams tweeted information in two broad categories: team building and team performance news. These tweets included information about players, the draft, new signees, and injury updates. To keep fans engaged and returning to the team's online space (conservation of visitors and generation of return visits), teams used Twitter to encourage fans to check out other social media sites including team podcasts and mobile apps. All of the teams in the analysis integrated sophisticated graphics and video content into their Twitter feed. Finally, to get fans to engage with the team (dialogic loop), teams created branded hashtags to represent the team and encouraged fans to create user-generated content. These strategies encouraged engagement without the added pressure of having to respond to individual requests. In fact, many teams featured content from fans in the form of retweets.

NOTES

1. Carolina Panthers [Panthers]. (2017, June 13). Michael Oher is back in Charlotte after reconnecting with the #Panthers More Info [Tweet]. Retrieved from https://twitter.com/Panthers/status/874617191060185088/photo/1

2. Arizona Cardinals [AZCardinals]. (2017, May 23). Larry Fitzgerald discusses when he will address his future. [Tweet]. Retrieved from https://twitter.com/AZCardinals/status/867038315039473664

3. San Francisco Giants [SFGiants]. (2017, June 19). Buster Posey continues to pace NL catchers in All-Star balloting. Help keep him on top: sfgiants.com/vote #BustTheVote #SFGiants. [Tweet]. Retrieved from https://twitter.com/i/web/status/876886359692107776

4. San Francisco Giants [SFGiants]. (2017, June 16). ICYMI: Austin Slater recorded a career-best four hits last night and now has 12 hits in his last five games. #SFGiants. [Tweet]. Retrieved from https://twitter.com/i/web/status/875771649009647616

5. #LAKings [LAKings]. (2017, June 18). The LA Kings protected 9 players from being selected in the Expansion Draft by the Vegas Golden Knights. [Tweet]. Retrieved from https://twitter.com/LAKings/status/876620559739695104

6. ColumbusBlueJackets [BlueJacketsNHL]. (2017, June 18). The protected and available #CBJ players ahead of this week's expansion draft [Tweet]. Retrieved from https://twitter.com/bluejacketsnhl/status/876450793074896897

7. Dallas Stars [DallasStars]. (2017, June 21). The @GoldenKnights have selected Cody Eakin as their pick from the Dallas Stars in the Expansion Draft. Best of luck, Cody! #VegasDraft [Tweet]. Retrieved from https://twitter.com/i/web/status/877686629347053568

8. Dallas Stars [DallasStars]. (2017, June 19). Our protected list is out, and @OwenNewkirk provides some insight on why certain players were protected and others were not. [Tweet]. Retrieved from https://twitter.com/i/web/status/876912921728634881

9. Mariners [Mariners]. (2017, June 16). "We got a player in mind that we're hopin' to get..." Go inside the Mariners Draft Room for the selection of @Ewhite_19. [Tweet]. Retrieved from https://twitter.com/i/web/status/875831358169399296

10. #LAKings [LAKings]. (2017, June 7). The LA Kings re-sign Tyler Toffoli to a three-year contract with $4.6 million AAV. [Tweet]. Retrieved from https://twitter.com/lakings/status/872601695296962560

11. Arizona Cardinals [AZCardinals]. (2017, May 25). We've signed our second-round pick, @buddabaker32, to his rookie contract. READ [Tweet]. Retrieved from https://twitter.com/AZCardinals/status/867823260842336256/photo/1

12. Atlanta Falcons [AtlantaFalcons]. (2017, June 2). TRANSACTION: We have signed WR Marvin Hall and have waived OL Robert Leff. [Tweet]. Retrieved from https://twitter.com/atlantafalcons/status/870698066247995392

13. Dallas Mavericks [dallasmavs]. (2017, May 18). Mavericks may look at upgrading at the point guard position with their top-10 draft pick. @BBVACompass REPORT: go.mavs.com/l/5pg [Tweet]. Retrieved from https://twitter.com/i/web/status/865237016346214400

14. Mariners [Mariners]. (2017, June 21). Making the rounds. Welcome to Seattle, @samcarlson33! [Tweet]. Retrieved from https://twitter.com/Mariners/status/877668514160676864/photo/1

15. #LAKings [LAKings]. (2017, June 1). Welcome to LA, Bokondji Imama! [Tweet]. Retrieved from https://twitter.com/LAKings/status/870384670084431872

16. Atlanta Hawks [ATLHawks]. It's official. RETWEET to welcome @milesplumlee13 and @marcobelinelli to Atlanta! #TrueToAtlanta [Tweet]. Retrieved from https://twitter.com/ATLHawks/status/877504122814988288/photo/1

17. CarolinaPanthers [Panthers]. (2017, June 20). First look at @CMcCaffrey5 in black & blue. [Tweet]. Retrieved from https://twitter.com/Panthers/status/877241249618644992/photo/1

18. GoldenStateWarriors [warriors]. (2017, June 21). A look back on one of the more impressive & entertaining seasons in NBA history on.nba.com/2sonzbd. [Tweet]. Retrieved from https://twitter.com/warriors/status/877562782811439106/photo/1

19. AtlantaFalcons [AtlantaFalcons]. (2017, June 4). We split our series against the Bucs last year. What weapons has Tampa Bay has [*sic*] added since then? Scouting Report: atlfal.com.nz/2sEF17r [Tweet]. Retrieved from https://twitter.com/i/web/status/871488726224031745

20. Arizona Cardinals [AZCardinals]. (2017, June 9). @Cardschatter's nine takeaways from the offseason program bit.ly/takeways060917. [Tweet]. Retrieved from https://twitter.com/AZCardinals/status/873266231373029376/photo/1

21. Atlanta Falcons [AtlantaFalcons]. (2017, June 14). If you don't bring enough burst to practice, DQ will be the first to tell you. FULL Mic'd Up atlfal.co.nz/2rialKh. [Tweet]. Retrieved from https://twitter.com/i/web/status/875111879089152000

22. Atlanta Hawks [ATLHawks]. (2017, June 14). Today's pre-draft workouts include many recognizable faces! The complete roundup: on.nba.com/2tllv00 [Tweet]. Retrieved from https://twitter.com/ATLHawks/status/874986315493900288/photo/1

23. Dallas Mavericks [dallasmavs]. (2017, May 12). Tune in to FB live during the 2 o'clock hour to watch our very own @MavsChamp rappel down @ReunionTower #ShatterproofChallenge #MFFL [Tweet]. Retrieved from https://twitter.com/i/web/status/863045635389489153

24. Arizona Cardinals [AZCardinals]. (2017, June 21). Later today, join our team president Michael Bidwill for a LIVE Q&A on @NFLUK's Periscope. [Tweet]. Retrieved from https://twitter.com/AZCardinals/status/877528949768593408/photo/1

25. #LAKings [LAKings]. (2017, June 19). New @KingsMenPodcast! @lakingsinsider joins Cohen to break down the LA Kings' protected list for the Expansion Draft. [Tweet]. Retrieved from https://twitter.com/LAKings/status/876786649853591553

26. Dallas Mavericks [dallasmavs]. (2017, June 2). @matrix31 & @DannyBMFFL make their predictions for the NBA Finals in epi. 17 "That's what's up" podcast! LISTEN: go.mavs.com/l.5t0 [Tweet]. Retrieved from https://twitter.com/i/web/status/870672818169458688

27. Mariners [Mariners]. (2017, June 21). .@MarinersPod is a can't-miss today. All the audio from last night's walk-off win: Mariners.com/Podcast. [Tweet]. Retrieved from https://twitter.com/Mariners/status/877562940404060160/photo/1

28. #LAKings [LAKings]. (2017, May 12). Stay connected with other LA Kings fans and get exclusive content with the Kings Fans App! LAKings.com/Vixlet. [Tweet]. Retrieved from https://twitter.com/LAKings/status/863076307931873281/photo/1

29. CarolinaPanthers [Panthers]. (2017, June 12). We'll make your Monday morning more fun! Tune in to the debut of Captain's Corner, starring @captain_41! [Tweet]. Retrieved from https://twitter.com/Panthers/status/874247798316716033

30. Dallas Mavericks [dallasmavs]. (2017, June 6). @swish41 talked Barnes, Noel, the draft, his 19th season, and more Monday with Ben & Skin! LISTEN: go.mavs.com/l/5vX [Tweet]. Retrieved from https://twitter.com/i/web/status/872112482004881408

31. Mariners [Mariners]. (2017, June 20). You know Ben Gamel's wild catch made the cut. What else is in the #DidYouSeaThat Plays of the Week? Just watch. [Tweet]. Retrieved from https://twitter.com/Mariners/status/877323032292859904/video/1

32. ColumbusBlueJackets [BlueJacketsNHL]. (2017, June 13). "I almost got decapitated!" The best moments from #CBJ mic'd up this season [Tweet]. Retrieved from https://twitter.com/BlueJacketsNHL/status/874708965946384384/video/1

33. San Francisco Giants [SFGiants]. (2017, June 11). A fresh look at @BusterPosey's rally-starting double in the 7th #SFGiants #BustTheVote [Tweet]. Retrieved from https://twitter.com/SFGiants/status/874059653939965952/video/1

34. Atlanta Hawks [ATLHawks]. (2017, June 20). Can you name all of our first round draft picks since 2000? Try here: on.nba.com/2rAgGRP. [Tweet]. Retrieved from https://twitter.com/ATLHawks/status/877296757058699264/photo/1

35. Atlanta Hawks [ATLHawks]. (2017, June 9). What 3 all-time Hawks would you have on your 3-on-3 Olympic team? [Tweet]. Retrieved from https://twitter.com/ATLHawks/status/873233117573767171/photo/1

36. #LAKings [LAKings]. (2017, June 18). Show us how you celebrated your dad today by posting in the "My Hockey Dad" capsule on the LA Kings Fans App! >vxl.me/FathersDay2017 [Tweet] Retrieved from https://twitter.com/i/web/status/876650757897863169

37. #LAKings [LAKings]. (2017, June 7). Beat Bailey's 23 squats and post your video with #FitToBeKing to win @24hourfitness and Lenny & Larry prizes! LAKings.com/FTBKChallenge. [Tweet]. Retrieved from https://twitter.com/i/web/status/872498407490732032

38. Houston Astros [astros]. (2017, June 21). Another day, another chance to win a #VoteAstros t-shirt! Reply to this tweet with your ballot for a chance to win! Astros.com/Vote. [Tweet]. Retrieved from https://twitter.com/i/web/status/877573437446737921

39. Houston Astros [astros]. (2017, June 16). Share photos of you and your Astros fan kid/father/father figure using #AstrosDadDay for a chance to win a Father's Day prize pack! [Tweet]. Retrieved from https://twitter.com/i/web/status/875729719597170688

Chapter 7

Recommendations

The nature of sport as a service brand and its dependence on fans for support means that sport brands must develop strategies to build, enhance, and maintain a positive relationship with fans. Moreover, sport brands are realizing the impact they have on their communities (Summers and Morgan 2008), thus making relationship building with fans and the local community a priority for teams. A strong relationship between the sport fan and team has benefits for both parties. Through identification a sport team, a fan can satisfy their need for belonging with a social group and through team success can experience a boost in their self-esteem. For the sport fan, identification with their favorite team can become a self-defining feature especially when fans feel a self-brand connection with the team. From the team perspective, a strong fan-team relationship can have financial benefits including purchasing tickets and team licensed memorabilia. Beyond that, the loyalty exhibited by fans can carry a team through losing seasons.

Brands, including sport brands, that are able to master the dynamics of social media to establish a strong presence are better equipped to garner consumer attention, increase brand awareness, and maintain communication with consumers (Kwon and Sung 2011). Social media is about relationships, even for consumer and brand interactions. Opportunities for consumer-brand engagement is what sets social media apart from other marketing strategies. The interactive nature of the medium allows fans direct access to teams, which allows them to get information and interact with teams and athletes in ways not possible before social media. Active online engagement with fans constitutes an online relationship with the team where fan activity represents buy-in from fans. However, research presented in the literature has yet to go beyond conceptualizing engagement to examine the effectiveness of engagement for meeting relationship-building objectives. The research presented in this book is one step toward establishing a better understanding of how to use social media, and Twitter in particular, as a relationship-building tool.

Online engagement among fans can vary, and as evidenced in chapter 3, approaches to measuring online engagement can vary as well. Measuring engagement as a behavioral construct includes moving consumers along a continuum of lower levels of engagement (e.g., consuming content) to moderate levels of engagement (e.g., contributing content) to higher levels of engagement (e.g., creating content). Still others measure engagement as a cognitive/affective construct focusing on the results of engagement—thinking about the team, feelings toward the team as a result of engagement, and willingness to expend time and resources engaging online with the team.

Results of a survey of sport fans revealed that both approaches do, in fact, have a significant influence on fan-team relationship as well as other relationship-related outcomes. Moreover, consuming Twitter content and affective engagement were found to be the most influential in terms of meeting relationship-building goals using Twitter. The finding that affective engagement with the team on Twitter is important because it reiterates the value of the emotional connection fans have with their favorite team. Scholars in relationship and services marketing have noted the significance of the emotional connection between consumers and brands (Berry 2000; Morgan-Thomas, and Veloutsou 2013). The findings from this study reiterate the value of emotional involvement with the sport brand as a driving influence on the fan-team relationship. As such, sport brands should use social media to create opportunities for the enhancement of this emotional connection as a way to strengthen the fan-team bond.

The consuming content finding is significant for two reasons. First, initially social media was touted as a revolution in marketing because of the two-way communication capabilities. The findings of this study do not refute two-way communication as an important component of social media marketing, but what it does is contribute to the growing body of research that finds brands should not overlook the value of providing fans with access to information. In a sport context, this means providing fans with information related to the team, helping them connect with their favorite athletes, and keeping the team top of mind. These strategies have potential to be as effective as two-way communication between the fan and the team. However, understanding the extent to which these strategies help achieve the same goal is beyond the scope of the research presented here. The second reason this finding is significant is that it serves as a reminder to be strategic and intentional about content created by brands for social media. If the act of consuming content on Twitter can have positive benefits for the brand, then brands need to be even more aware of content that is provided and should take care that content meets the informational, entertainment, and interactive needs of the user. Thus, making it even more important to listen to fans and provide Twitter content that meets their needs.

Given that consuming content was found to be a significant influence on the fan-team relationship, it was important then to analyze and organize content produced by professional sport teams. Within the literature there are countless studies that content analyze the content produced by various organizations using social media. Much of these studies utilize quantitative methods and fit content into prescribed categories. The research presented in chapters 4, 5, and 6 implemented qualitative methods using thematic analysis to identify existing content strategies employed by professional sport teams. Strategies were identified based on theoretical concepts related to brand personality, celebrity relationship culture, and dialogue. Findings from this research is summarized in table 7.1.

The research in this book set out to establish that online engagement is an effective relationship-building tool. The second half of this book revealed the content strategies implemented by professional sport teams on social media. As evidenced in table 7.1, teams employ a variety of content strategies on Twitter. The next step for scholarly research on engagement, is to test the effectiveness of these strategies on the perception of fan-team relationship. This research will provide insight into whether or not communicating team history or integrating social media platforms are more effective. Perhaps it is a combination of content strategies that provides the most effective tool for relationship building. Furthermore, research is needed to better under-stand the connection between how engagement is measured, on behavioral dimensions or cognitive/affective dimensions, and effective relationship-building strategies.

RECOMMENDATIONS

There is no shortage of research possibilities as it relates to online engagement and consumer-brand relationship-building efforts. The research presented in this book provides a starting point for continued scholarly inquiry into this topic. There are, however, practical applications that can be gleaned from the research findings presented in the previous chapters. More specifically, practitioners should (1) be strategic about content creation, (2) create content that sparks and emotional connection with fans, and (3) take a comprehensive approach to measuring online engagement.

Table 7.1. Content Strategies from Chapters 4 through 6

	Strategies	*Tactics*
Brand Personality Chapter 4	brand associations	tweets with information related to jerseys, team venue, mascots, dance team
	personality congruence	tweets that include memes, popular culture references, holidays, and current events
	fan-team connections	Tweets with information related to the team history, togetherness and family, and hard work
Athletes Chapter 5	use players as team ambassadors	tweets that emphasize the celebrity of athletes, team promotional appearances, and community appearances
	features and profiles of athletes	tweets with links to feature stories and profiles about athletes; including personal information about players or updates about player status
	player preparation	tweets that show players training and working out in preparation for next season; show fans that players are serious about improvement
	player award and achievements	tweets that recognized and congratulated players for individual achievements
	birthdays	tweets that wish players a happy birthday; many encourage fans to retweet to wish player a happy birthday

	Strategies	*Tactics*
Dialogue Chapter 6	provide useful information	tweets that include team building news, such as player news, drafts, trades, and signings
		tweets that include information related to team performance, such as previews and recaps of seasons, information related to training camps
	employ conservation of visitors and generation of return visits principles	tweets that integrate other social media platforms
		tweets that include multimedia content
	encourage interaction	tweets utilize team specific branded hashtags
		tweets that encourage user-generated content

Be Strategic about Content Creation

As previously noted, consuming online brand content can have a positive influence on the fan-team relationship. Therefore, brands need to be strategic and purposeful about the content they create. For a brand to be successful on social media, they must find creative and effective strategies for engaging consumers (Johnston 2014). When using social media as a marketing tool, it is the brand's responsibility to initiate the relationship and create content that encourages consumer engagement (Culnan, McHugh, and Zubillag 2010). Research in sports communication suggests that team and fan identification can be strengthened by strategic communication from the team (Heere and James 2007) and consumers are more likely to react positively and engage with brands that are genuinely interested in developing a relationship with the consumer (Vivek, Beatty, and Morgan 2012). One strategy for doing this includes creating online content that aligns with the consumer's goals.

People are motivated by goals, and these goals often influence a person's decision to act in a situation (Higgins and Scholer 2009). When a consumer perceives a connection between the brand and their personal goals or values, then higher levels of engagement are likely to follow (Van Doorn et al. 2010), which subsequently can have a positive influence on the fan-team relationship. Therefore, it can be argued that when the offerings of a brand align with a person's goals, then they are going to be more likely to engage with that brand. For example, if a person aspires to be a runner, then they are going to be more likely to engage in online spaces sponsored by brands like Nike that will help the person achieve his or her goal of being a runner. As the person interacts with branded content in pursuit of his or her goal, then brand engagement behaviors are more likely to follow.

Create Content That Sparks an Emotional Connection with Fans

Findings from this research also reiterated the importance of having an emotional connection with fans. In the sport context, it is important for teams to show a high level of commitment to fans if they expect fans to identify and engage with them, which is necessary for relationship building. Sport fans tend to reciprocate such efforts (Pronschinske, Groza, and Walker 2012). Sports teams have harnessed the power of social media to convert casual fans to highly involved fans (Ioakamidis 2010). Active engagement with a team leads to increased levels of fan identification (Hambrick et al. 2010) and defining and connecting with athletes deepens the attachment to the team (Browning and Sanderson 2012). For highly identified fans, online sport websites and social media allow them to connect with their favorite athletes and gain insider information about the team (Seo and Green 2008). Meeting the information needs of sport fans is just a start. As research suggests, it is affective engagement that can have the biggest impact on the fan-team relationship. As such, teams should focus on the more emotional aspects of fandom, especially the need for belonging that is satisfied through sport fandom.

As discussed in the part I overview, sports are important because they bring people together. Through social identification, sport fans integrate the team into their personal identity to the point where fandom becomes a self-identifying feature. Moreover, being a sport fan is about more than cheering for a team, it is about feeling like you belong with a group of like-minded people; thus, making belonging a central part of sport fandom (Karjaluoto, Munnukka, and Salmi, 2016). Social media content that emphasizes this sense of belonging also capitalizes on the emotional connection fans have with a sport team, which can also enhance the fan-team relationship. Therefore, sport brands need to create content that is relative to the consumer and meets not only the informational needs but the sense of belonging that is exemplified through sport fandom.

Take a Comprehensive Approach to Measuring Engagement

It is the responsibility of the practitioners to better understand what drives consumers to use these tools and engage with the brand online (Bitter, Grabner-Krauter, and Breitenecker 2014). Knowing the attitudes and behaviors of committed fans can provide brand managers with insight into how to better present the sport product, communicate with fans more effectively, and predict fan consumption behavior (Fink, Trail, and Anderson 2002; Funk and James 2006). Scholarly research on engagement centers on the assumption that consumers are active participants with the brand (Hollebeek, Glynn, and Brodie 2014), but this can take different forms depending on how the brand defines and measures engagement. Results of the research presented within this book point to taking a more comprehensive approach to determining what constitutes online fan engagement. Different approaches to engagement classify it has a behavior or a cognitive/affective response, but results of this study indicate it can be both. Therefore, it is important for practitioners to have clearly defined goals for the Twitter and other social media content to determine the appropriate method for measuring engagement.

The level of fan engagement can vary over time and with brand experience (Brodie et al. 2011). Research has suggested that certain people are more predisposed to engaging with brands than others (Van Doorn et al. 2010), while still others suggest that some consumers are motivated to engage with a brand based on the benefits they expect to receive from brand engagement (Vivek, Beatty, and Morgan 2012). Attitude toward and engagement with a brand can change as the relationship between the consumer and the brand evolves (Van Doorn et al. 2010). A review of the research on motivations for engagement reveals three factors that influence engagement with a brand: (1) identification with a brand, (2) experience with a brand, and (3) consumer goal alignment with the brand. It is up to the sport brand to listen to fans and develop strategies that encourage specific forms of engagement.

This book has examined the use of Twitter as a relationship-building tool using mixed-methods scholarly research. Overall, the findings of the research presented in this book provide support for using Twitter as a tool to facilitate the fan-team relationship and identified the content strategies implemented by professional sport teams using Twitter. In conclusion, strong fan-team relationships have potential to be a truly mutually beneficial relationship. However, as with all manners of relationships, it takes work to maintain levels of closeness and interaction that sustains a relationship. This involves buy-in from both parties and a willingness to understand where the other is coming from. Social media, and Twitter in particular, can be a valuable tool for facilitating interactions and understanding in a relational context. To date, many sport brands have demonstrated various levels of success with using social media, and continued research into not only engagement, but also the effectiveness of content strategies can provide valuable insights for the continued development of fan-team relationships.

Appendix A

Survey Measures and Item Analysis

Table A.1. Survey Measures and Item Analysis

	α	M	SD
Fan-Team Relationship (Kim, Park, and Kim 2014)	.888	4.03	0.567
I feel at home with my favorite sport team		4.20	0.829
Being a fan of my favorite sports team adds a sense of stability		3.83	0.968
I feel safe and secure as a fan of my favorite sport team		4.16	0.826
It would be destructive, in some ways, if I have to select another sports team		3.66	1.100
I will stay with my favorite sports team through good times and bad		4.27	0.854
I have made a pledge to stick with my favorite sports team		4.14	0.937
I know things about my favorite sports team that many people just don't know		3.98	0.924
I know a lot about the organization that operates my favorite sports team		4.14	0.884
I feel as if I really understand my favorite sports team		4.12	0.878
My favorite sports team and I have a lot in common		3.89	0.913
My favorite sports team's image and my image are similar in a lot of ways		3.88	0.888

	α	M	SD
My favorite sports team says a lot about the kind of person I am or want to be		3.78	1.052
No other team can quite take the place of my favorite team		4.12	0.867
I have a powerful attraction to my favorite team		4.15	0.812
I have feelings for this team that I don't for many other teams		4.11	0.846

	α	M	SD
Self-Brand Connection (Escalas, 2004; Hollebeek et al., 2014)	.855	3.94	0.668
My favorite team reflects who I am		3.84	0.922
I can identify with my favorite sports team		4.07	0.856
I feel a personal connection to my favorite sports team		4.06	0.869
I use my sport fandom to communicate who I am to other people		3.83	0.973
I think being a sport fan could help me become the type of person I want to be		3.81	1.013
I consider my sport fandom to be "me" (it reflects who I consider myself to be or the way I want to present myself to others)		3.77	0.964
My favorite team suits me well		4.23	0.780

	α	M	SD
Loyalty (Mahony, Madrigal, and Howard, 2000)	.728	3.77	0.510
I might rethink my allegiance to my favorite team if this team consistently performs poorly		2.99	1.451
I would watch a game featuring my favorite team regardless of who they are playing		4.17	0.907
I would rethink my allegiance to my favorite team if management traded away its players		3.09	1.363
Being a fan of my favorite team is important to me		4.10	0.902
Nothing could change my allegiance to my favorite team		3.99	0.942
I am a committed fan of my favorite team		4.32	0.780
It would not affect my loyalty to my favorite team if management hired a head coach I disliked very much		3.78	1.040

	α	M	SD
I could easily be persuaded to change my favorite team preference		2.88	1.470
I have been a fan of my favorite team since I started watching sports		4.13	0.965
I could never switch my loyalty from my favorite team even if my close friends were fans of another team		4.17	0.926
It would be unlikely for me to change my allegiance from my current team to another		4.13	0.924
It would be difficult to change my beliefs about my favorite team		4.06	0.894
You can tell a lot about a person by their willingness to stick with a team that is not performing well		4.05	0.848
My commitment to my favorite team would decrease if they were performing poorly and there appeared little chance their performance would change		3.00	1.404

	α	M	SD
Behavioral Dimensions of Engagement (developed from Schiviniski, Christodoulides, and Dabrowski 2016)			
• Consume—Read Tweets	.866	3.72	0.834
I read tweets from my favorite team		3.79	1.053
I look at pictures/graphics of my favorite team on Twitter		3.75	1.003
I watch videos or gifs of my favorite team on Twitter		3.58	1.061
I read tweets from other sports fans about my favorite team on Twitter		3.68	1.030
I read tweets with information related my favorite team on Twitter		3.78	1.024
• Contribute—like tweets	0.905	3.48	0.981
I like tweets from my favorite team on Twitter		3.49	1.146
I like tweets with pictures/graphics of my favorite team on Twitter		3.46	1.146
I like tweets with videos or gifs of my favorite team on Twitter		3.51	1.164

	α	M	SD
I like tweets other fans write about my favorite team on Twitter		3.39	1.184
I like tweets with information about my favorite team on Twitter		3.55	1.119
• Contribute - Retweet	0.927	3.22	1.099
I retweet tweets from my favorite team on Twitter		3.25	1.252
I retweet tweets with pictures/graphics of my favorite team on Twitter		3.27	1.254
I retweet tweets with videos or gifs of my favorite team on Twitter		3.24	1.257
I retweet tweets from other fans about my favorite team		3.16	1.244
I retweet tweets with information about my favorite team on Twitter		3.20	1.240
• Create – Reply to Tweets	0.940	3.17	1.141
I reply to tweets from my favorite team on Twitter		3.19	1.277
I reply to tweets with pictures/graphics of my favorite team on Twitter		3.22	1.291
I reply to tweets with videos or gifs of my favorite team on Twitter		3.15	1.290
I reply to other fans' tweets about my favorite team on Twitter		3.11	1.238
I reply to tweets with information related to my favorite team on Twitter		3.20	1.262
• Create—Write Tweets	0.935	3.11	1.161
I write tweets to my favorite team on Twitter		3.14	1.312
I write tweets that include pictures/graphics of my favorite team on Twitter		3.13	1.304
I write tweets that include videos or gifs of my favorite team on Twitter		3.07	1.323
I write tweets to other fans about my favorite team on Twitter		3.07	1.298
I write tweets with information related to my favorite team on Twitter		3.14	1.280
	α	M	SD
Affective/Cognitive Dimensions of Engagement (developed from Hollebeek, Glynn, and Brodie 2014)	.855	3.94	0.668

	α	M	SD
• Cognitive Engagement	0.767	3.84	0.745
Using Twitter to follow sports gets me to think about my favorite team		3.92	0.852
I think about my favorite team a lot when I use Twitter to follow sports		3.74	0.939
Using Twitter to follow sports stimulates my interest to learn more about my favorite team		3.86	0.914
• Affective Engagement	0.845	3.92	0.729
I feel very positive when I use Twitter to follow my favorite sports team		3.95	0.858
Using Twitter to follow my favorite sport team makes me happy		3.97	0.877
I feel good when I use Twitter to follow my favorite sports team		3.87	0.888
I'm proud to use Twitter to follow my favorite sports team		3.88	0.908
• Activation Engagement	0.765	3.78	0.815
I spend a lot of time using Twitter to follow sports compared to other social media sites		3.68	1.047
Whenever I'm following sports online, I'm usually using Twitter		3.69	1.010
Twitter is one of the sources I use to get information about sports		3.97	0.901

* α = Chronbach's alpha, *M* = mean; *SD* = standard deviation

Appendix B

Behavioral Dimensions of Online Engagement Statistical Analysis

A multiple regression analysis and Pearson correlation were used to determine the influence of behavioral dimensions of engagement (consume, contribute, create) on loyalty to the team, self-brand connections with the team, and fan-team relationship. Assumptions related to the use of multiple regression were examined for each variable. Independence of residuals was assessed using the Durbin Watson statistic, and all tests had values of approximately 2.00. Homoscedacity was assessed by visual inspection of a plot of standardized residuals versus standardized predicted values and normal distribution was assessed through visual inspection of a normal probability plot. Each of the assumptions for the proper execution for the multiple regression analysis was met. The independent variables for each analysis was (1) reading tweets—consume, (2) like and retweet—contribute, and (3) reply and write tweets—create. The dependent variables for the analysis was (a) loyalty, (b) self-brand connection, and (c) fan-team relationship.

Results indicated support for each model and thus provided support for the behavioral dimensions of engagement leading to positive brand-related outcomes. More specifically, the multiple regression model statistically significantly predicted loyalty, $F(5, 344) = 45.820$, $p<.001$, adj. $R^2 = .391$; self-brand connection, $F(5, 349) = 25.688$, $p<.001$, adj. $R^2 = .259$; and fan-team relationship, $F(5, 344) = 20.049$, $p<.001$, adj. $R^2 = .215$. Table B.1 summarizes these findings.

A closer look at the analysis revealed that for loyalty, reading tweets ($\beta = .265$) and writing tweets ($\beta = .354$) had a significant, low-to-moderate influence on loyalty while reading tweets was the only significant individual influence on self-brand connection ($\beta = .186$) and fan-team relationship ($\beta = .354$). This indicates that having access to online content about the team can be positive for the sport brand.

Table B.1. Summary of Multiple Regression Analysis—Behavioral Dimension of Online Engagement

Dependent Variable – Loyalty			
Variable	B	SEB	β
Intercept	2.498	0.096	
read tweets	0.159	0.036	0.265*
like tweets	0.056	0.053	-0.088
retweet	0.038	0.042	0.109
reply to tweets	-0.039	0.056	0.083
write tweets	0.154	0.049	0.354*
Dependent Variable – Self-Brand Connection			
Variable	B	SEB	β
Intercept	2.523	0.141	
read tweets	0.15	0.053	0.186*
like tweets	0.151	0.061	0.220*
retweet	0.09	0.081	0.147
reply to tweets	-0.036	0.076	-0.062
write tweets	0.053	0.072	0.09
Dependent Variable – Fan-Team Relationship			
Variable	B	SEB	β
Intercept	2.829	0.124	
read tweets	0.242	0.046	.354*
like tweets	0.063	0.053	0.108
retweet	0.047	0.071	0.09
reply to tweets	-0.038	0.068	-0.077
write tweets	0.02	0.063	0.04

*$p < .05$; B = unstandardized regression coefficient; SEB = standardized coefficient error; β = standardized coefficient

Appendix C

Cognitive/Affective Dimensions of Online Engagement Statistical Analysis

To evaluate the effectiveness of the cognitive/affective component of engagement, a second multiple regression analysis was conducted. Similar to the previous analysis, assumptions related to the use of multiple regression were examined for each variable. Independence of residuals was assessed using the Durbin Watson statistic, and all tests had values of approximately 2.00. Homoscedacity was assessed by visual inspection of a plot of standardized residuals versus standardized predicted values and normal distribution was assessed through visual inspection of a normal probability plot. Each of the assumptions for the proper execution for the multiple regression analysis was met. The independent variables for each analysis were (1) cognitive engagement, (2) affective engagement, and (3) activation engagement with the team.

Results of this analysis provide support for the model and indicate that the cognitive/affective components of engagement can also result in positive brand-related outcomes. More specifically, the multiple regression model statistically significantly predicted loyalty, $F(3, 356) = 62.695$, $p<.001$, adj. $R^2 = .340$; self-brand connection, $F(3, 364) = 67.007$, $p<.001$, adj. $R^2 = .350$; and fan-team relationship, $F(3, 354) = 72.788$, $p<.001$, adj. $R^2 = .376$. These findings support the cognitive/affective dimensions of engagement as having a positive influence on factors that support a positive fan-team relationship.

A closer look at the analysis revealed that for loyalty, cognitive ($\beta = .232$) and affective ($\beta = .236$) engagement had a significant but low influence on team loyalty. Affective engagement with the team, or the positive feelings toward the team, had a significant and moderate influence on self-brand connection ($\beta = .475$) and fan-team relationship ($\beta = .575$). Table C.1 summarizes these findings.

Table C.1. Summary of Multiple Regression Analysis—Cognitive/Behavioral Dimension of Online Engagement

		Dependent Variable – Loyalty	
Variable	B	SEB	β
Intercept	2.095	0.124	
cognitive engagement	0.159	0.05	.232*
affective engagement	0.164	0.051	0.236*
activation engagement	0.113	0.038	0.182*

		Dependent Variable – Self-Brand Connection	
Variable	B	SEB	β
Intercept	1.729	0.160	
cognitive engagement	0.1	0.064	0.112
affective engagement	0.434	0.067	.475*
activation engagement	0.033	0.05	0.04

		Dependent Variable – Fan-Team Relationship	
Variable	B	SEB	β
Intercept	2.132	0.135	
cognitive engagement	0.003	0.054	0.003
affective engagement	0.444	0.055	.575*
activation engagement	0.039	0.042	0.056

*$p < .05$; B = unstandardized regression coefficient; SEB = standardized coefficient error; β = standardized coefficient

References

Aaker, Jennifer L. 1997. "Dimensions of Brand Personality." *Journal of Marketing Research,* 34 no. 3: 347–56.

Aaker, Jennifer, Susan Fournier, and S. Adam Braseal. 2004. "When Good Brands Do Bad." *Journal of Consumer Research* 31, no. 1: 1–16.

Abeza, Gashaw, and Norm O'Reilly. 2014. "Social Media Platforms Use in Building Stakeholder Relationships: The Case of National Sport Organizations." *Journal of Applied Sport Management* 6, no. 3: 103–26.

Abeza, Gashaw, Norm O'Reilly, and Ian Reid. 2013. "Relationship Marketing and Social Media in Sport." *International Journal of Sport Communication* 6, no. 2: 120–142.

AgencyCSE. "Tinder Night, or Swipe Right Night at the Atlanta Hawks." YouTube. April 24, 2015. Accessed April 1, 2018. https://www.youtube.com/watch?v=vs7n_5f_CPs.

Aggarwal, Pankaj. 2004. "The Effects of Brand Relationship Norms on Consumer Attitudes and Behavior." *Journal of Consumer Research* 31, no. 1: 87–101.

Agyemang, Kwame JA, and Antonio S. Williams. 2016. "Managing Celebrity via Impression Management on Social Network Sites: An Exploratory Study of NBA Celebrity Athletes." *Sport, Business and Management: An International Journal* 6, no. 4: 440–59.

Anderson, Lars. "Terror, Tragedy and Hope in Tuscaloosa." SI.com. May 23, 2011. Accessed May 15, 2018. https://www.si.com/vault/2011/05/23/106070645/terror-tragedy-and-hope-in-tuscaloosa.

Arvidsson, Adam. 2006. *Brands: Meaning and Value in Media Culture.* New York: Routledge.

Ashforth, Blake E., and Fred Mael. 1989. "Social Identity Theory and the Organization." *Academy of Management Review* 14, no. 1: 20–39.

Badenhausen, Kurt. "Full List: The World's 50 Most Valuable Sports Teams 2017." Forbes. July 14, 2017. Accessed May 15, 2018. https://www.forbes.com/sites/

kurtbadenhausen/2017/07/12/full-list-the-worlds-50-most-valuable-sports-teams-2017/#206bce64a05c.

Balakrishnan, Anita, and Julia Boorstin. "Instagram Says It Now Has 800 Million Users, Up 100 Million since April." CNBC. September 25, 2017. Accessed June 15, 2018. https://www.cnbc.com/2017/09/25/how-many-users-does-instagram-have-now-800-million.html.

Batra, R., D. R. Lehmann, & D. Singh. 1993. "The Brand Personality Component of Brand Goodwill: Some Antecedents and Consequences." In *Brand Equity and Advertising: Advertising's Role in Building Strong Brands*, edited by David A. Aaker and Alexander L. Biel, 83–96. Hillsdale, NJ: Lawrence Erlbaum Associates.

Bee, Colleen C., and Lynn R. Kahie. 2006. "Relationship Marketing in Sports: A Functional Approach." *Sport Marketing Quarterly* 15, no. 2: 102–10.

Bergami, Massimo, and Richard P. Bagozzi. 2000. "Self-Categorization, Affective Commitment and Group Self-Esteem as Distinct Aspects of Social Identity in the Organization." *British Journal of Social Psychology* 39, no. 4: 555–77.

Berry, Leonard L. 1995. "Relationship Marketing of Services—Growing Interest, Emerging Perspectives." *Journal of the Academy of Marketing Science* 23, no. 4: 236–45.

Berry, Leonard L. 2000. "Cultivating Service Brand Equity." *Journal of the Academy of Marketing Science* 28, no. 1: 128–37.

Bhattacharya, Chitrabhan B., and Sankar Sen. 2003. "Consumer-Company Identification: A Framework for Understanding Consumers' Relationships with Companies." *Journal of Marketing* 67, no. 2: 76–88.

Biel, A. L., 1993. "Converting Image into Equity." In *Brand Equity and Advertising: Advertising's Role in Building Strong Brands*, edited by David A. Aaker and Alexander L. Biel, 67–82. Hillsdale, NJ: Lawrence Erlbaum Associates.

Bitter, Sofie, Sonja Grabner-Kräuter, and Robert J. Breitenecker. 2014. "Customer Engagement Behaviour in Online Social Networks–the Facebook Perspective." *International Journal of Networking and Virtual Organisations* 14, no. 1–2: 197–220.

Bortree, Denise Servick, and Trent Seltzer. 2009. "Dialogic Strategies and Outcomes: An Analysis of Environmental Advocacy Groups' Facebook Profiles." *Public Relations Review* 35, no. 3: 317–19.

Bodet, Guillaume, and Iouri Bernache-Assollant. 2011. "Consumer Loyalty in Sport Spectatorship Services: The Relationships with Consumer Satisfaction and Team Identification." *Psychology & Marketing* 28, no. 8: 781–802.

Boyd, Danah, and Nicole Ellison. 2007. "Social Network Sites: Definition, History, and Scholarship." *Journal of Computer-Mediated Communication* 13, no. 1: 210–30.

Boyd, Thomas C., and Matthew D. Shank. 2004. "Athletes as Product Endorsers: The Effect of Gender and Product Relatedness." *Sport Marketing Quarterly* 13, no. 2: 82–93.

Boyle, Brett A., and Peter Magnusson. 2007. "Social Identity and Brand Equity Formation: A Comparative Study of Collegiate Sports fans." *Journal of Sport Management* 21, no. 4: 497–520.

Branscombe, Nyla R., and Daniel L. Wann. 1991. "The Positive Social and Self-Concept Consequences of Sports Team Identification." *Journal of Sport and Social Issues* 15, no. 2: 115–27.

Branscombe, Nyla R., and Daniel L. Wann. 1992. "Role of Identification with a Group, Arousal, Categorization Processes, and Self-Esteem in Sports Spectator Aggression." *Human Relations* 45, no. 10: 1013–33.

Braunstein, J. R. and J. J. Zhang. 2005. Dimensions of Athletic Star Power Associated with Generation Y Sports Consumption. *International Journal of Sports Marketing and Sponsorship* 6, no. 4: 37–62.

Braunstein, Jessica R., and Stephen D. Ross. 2010. "Brand Personality in Sport: Dimension Analysis and General Scale Development." *Sport Marketing Quarterly* 19, no. 1 (2010): 8–16.

Brodie, Roderick J., Linda D. Hollebeek, Biljana Jurić, and Ana Ilić. 2011. "Customer Engagement: Conceptual Domain, Fundamental Propositions, and Implications for Research." *Journal of Service Research* 14, no. 3: 252–71.

Broom, G. M., S. Casey, and J. Ritchey. 1997. Toward a Concept and Theory of Organization-Public Relationships. *Journal of Public Relations Research* 9, no. 2: 83–98.

Brown, Rupert. 2000. "Social Identity Theory: Past Achievements, Current Problems, and Future Challenges." *European Journal of Social Psychology* 30, no. 6: 745–778.

Browning, Blair, and Jimmy Sanderson. 2012. "The Positives and Negatives of Twitter: Exploring How Student-Athletes Use Twitter and Respond to Critical Tweets." *International Journal of Sport Communication* 5, no. 4: 503–21.

Bruning, Stephen D., Melissa Dials, and Amanda Shirka. 2008. "Using Dialogue to Build Organization–Public Relationships, Engage Publics, and Positively Affect Organizational Outcomes." *Public Relations Review* 34, no. 1: 25–31.

Carlson, Brad D., and D. Todd Donavan. 2008. "Concerning the Effect of Athlete Endorsements on Brand and Team-Related Intentions." *Sport Marketing Quarterly* 17, no. 3: 154–62.

———. 2013. "Human Brands in Sport: Athlete Brand Personality and Identification." *Journal of Sport Management* 27, no. 3: 193–206.

Carlson, Brad D., D. Todd Donavan, and Kevin J. Cumiskey. 2009. "Consumer-Brand Relationships in Sport: Brand Personality and Identification." *International Journal of Retail & Distribution Management* 37, no. 4: 370–84.

Christian, Julie, Richard Bagozzi, Dominic Abrams, and Harriet Rosenthal. 2012. "Social Influence in Newly Formed Groups: The Roles of Personal and Social Intentions, Group Norms, and Social Identity." *Personality and Individual Differences* 52, no. 3: 255–60.

Christodoulides, George, Colin Jevons, and Jennifer Bonhomme. 2012. "Memo to Marketers: Quantitative Evidence for Change." *Journal of Advertising Research* 52, no. 1: 53–64.

Clavio, Galen, and Ted M. Kian. 2010. "Uses and Gratifications of a Retired Female Athlete's Twitter Followers." *International Journal of Sport Communication* 3, no. 4: 485–500.

Clavio, Galen, and Patrick Walsh. 2014. "Dimensions of Social Media Utilization among College Sport Fans." *Communication & Sport* 2, no. 3: 261–81.

Cliffe, Simon J., and Judy Motion. 2005. "Building Contemporary Brands: A Sponsorship-Based Strategy." *Journal of Business Research* 58, no. 8: 1068–77.

Coffey, Amanda, and Paul Atkinson. 1996. *Making Sense of Qualitative Data: Complimentary Research Strategies.* Thousand Oaks, CA: Sage

"Company Info." Facebook Newsroom. 2018. Accessed January 6, 2018. https://newsroom.fb.com/company-info/.

Cousens, Laura, Kathy Babiak, and Trevor Slack. 2001. "Adopting a Relationship Marketing Paradigm: The Case of the National Basketball Association." *International Journal of Sports Marketing and Sponsorship* 2, no. 4: 60–84.

Couvelaere, Vincent, and André Richelieu. 2005. "Brand Strategy in Professional Sports: The Case of French Soccer Teams." *European Sport Management Quarterly* 5, no. 1: 23–46.

Cresswell, John W. 2007. *Qualitative Inquiry and Research Design: Choosing among Five Approaches* (2nd ed.). Thousand Oaks: CA: Sage.

Culnan, Mary J., Patrick J. McHugh, and Jesus I. Zubillaga. 2010. "How Large US Companies Can Use Twitter and Other Social Media to Gain Business Value." *MIS Quarterly Executive* 9, no. 4: 243–59.

De Chernatony, Leslie, and Francesca Dall'Olmo Riley. 1999. "Experts' Views about Defining Service Brands and the Principles of Services Branding." *Journal of Business Research* 46, no. 2: 181–92.

DiMoro, Anthony. "The Growing Impact of Social Media on Today's Sports Culture." Forbes. July 02, 2015. Accessed February 23, 2018. https://www.forbes.com/sites/anthonydimoro/2015/07/02/the-growing-impact-of-social-media-on-todays-sports-culture/2/#6e2094f6d68b.

DiStaso, Marcia W., Tina McCorkindale, and Donald K. Wright. 2011. "How Public Relations Executives Perceive and Measure the Impact of Social Media in Their Organizations." *Public Relations Review* 37, no. 3: 325–28.

Donavan, D. Todd, Brad D. Carlson, and Mickey Zimmerman. 2005. "The Influence of Personality Traits on Sports Fan Identification." *Sport Marketing Quarterly* 14, no. 1: 31–42.

Dwyer, Brendan, Gregory P. Greenhalgh, and Carrie W. LeCrom. 2015. "Exploring Fan Behavior: Developing a Scale to Measure Sport eFANgelism." *Journal of Sport Management* 29, no. 6: 642–56.

Effing, Robin, and Ton A. M. Spil. 2016. "The Social Strategy Cone: Towards a Framework for Evaluating Social Media Strategies. *International Journal of Information Management,* 36: 1–8.

Ellemers, N., and S. Alexander Haslem. 2011. "Social Identity Theory." In *Handbook of Theories of Social Psychology,* edited by Paul A. M. Van Lange, Arie W. Kruglanski, and E. Tory Higgins, 379–98. Los Angeles, CA: Sage.

Enginkaya, Ebru, and Hakan Yılmaz. 2014. "What Drives Consumers to Interact with Brands through Social Media? A Motivation Scale Development Study." *Procedia-Social and Behavioral Sciences* 148: 219–26.

Feng, Wei, and Jianyong Wang. 2014. "We Can Learn Your #hashtags: Connecting Tweets to ExplicitTtopics." In *Data Engineering (ICDE), 2014 IEEE 30th International Conference on Data Engineering*, Mar. 31 – Apr. 4 Chicago, IL, pp. 856–67. IEEE.

Filo, Kevin, Daniel Lock, and Adam Karg. "2015. Sport and Social Media Research: A Review." *Sport Management Review* 18, no. 2: 166–81.

Fink, Janet S., Heidi M. Parker, Martin Brett, and Julie Higgins. 2009. "Off-Field Behavior of Athletes and Team Identification: Using Social Identity Theory and Balance Theory to Explain Fan Reactions." *Journal of Sport Management* 23, no. 2: 142–55.

Fink, Janet S., Galen T. Trail, and Dean F. Anderson. 2002. "An Examination of Team Identification: Which Motives Are Most Salient to Its Existence?" *International Sports Journal* 6, no. 2: 195–207.

Fournier, Susan. 1998. "Consumers and Their Brands: Developing Relationship Theory in Consumer Research." *Journal of Consumer Research* 24, no. 4: 343–73.

Fournier, Susan, and Claudio Alvarez. 2012. "Brands as Relationship Partners: Warmth, Competence, and In-Between." *Journal of Consumer Psychology* 22, no. 2: 177–85.

Fournier, Susan, and Julie L. Yao. 1997. "Reviving Brand Loyalty: A Reconceptualization within the Framework of Consumer-Brand Relationships." *International Journal of Research in Marketing* 14, no. 5: 451–72.

Frederick, Evan, Marion E. Hamrick, and Galen Clavio. 2014. "Bypass and Broadcast: Utilizing Parasocial Interaction to Examine @NHL Communication on Twitter During the 2012–2013 Lockout." *Journal of Sports Media* 9, no. 2: 25–44.

Frederick, Evan, Choong Hoon Lim, Galen Clavio, Paul M. Pedersen, and Lauren M. Burch. 2014. "Choosing Between the One-Way or Two-Way Street: An Exploration of Relationship Promotion by Professional Athletes on Twitter." *Communication & Sport* 2, no. 1: 80–99.

Frederick, Evan L., Choong Hoon Lim, Galen Clavio, and Patrick Walsh. 2012. "Why We Follow: An Examination of Parasocial Interaction and Fan Motivations for Following Athlete Archetypes on Twitter." *International Journal of Sport Communication* 5, no. 4: 481–502.

Freling, Traci H., Jody L. Crosno, and David H. Henard. 2011. "Brand Personality Appeal: Conceptualization and Empirical Validation." *Journal of the Academy of Marketing Science* 39, no. 3: 392–406.

Funk, Daniel C., and Jeff James. 2001. "The Psychological Continuum Model: A Conceptual Framework for Understanding an Individual's Psychological Connection to Sport." *Sport Management Review* 4, no. 2: 119–50.

———. 2006. "Consumer Loyalty: The Meaning of Attachment in the Development of Sport Team Allegiance." *Journal of Sport Management* 20, no. 2: 189–217.

Funk, Daniel C., Lynn L. Ridinger, and Anita M. Moorman. 2004. "Exploring Origins of Involvement: Understanding the Relationship between Consumer Motives and Involvement with Professional Sport Teams." *Leisure Sciences* 26, no. 1: 35–61.

Gantz, Walter, and Nicky Lewis. 2014. "Fanship Differences between Traditional and Newer Media." In *Routledge Handbook of Sport and New Media,* edited by A. C. Billings and M. Hardin, 19–31. New York: Routledge.

Gensler, Sonja, Franziska Völckner, Yuping Liu-Thompkins, and Caroline Wiertz. 2013. "Managing Brands in the Social Media Environment." *Journal of Interactive Marketing* 27, no. 4: 242–56.

Geurin-Eagleman, Andrea N., and Lauren M. Burch. 2016. "Communicating via Photographs: A Gendered Analysis of Olympic Athletes' Visual Self-Presentation on Instagram." *Sport Management Review* 19, no. 2: 133–45.

Gladden, James M., and Daniel C. Funk. 2002. "Developing an Understanding of Brand Associations in Team Sport: Empirical Evidence from Consumers of Professional Sport." *Journal of Sport Management* 16, no. 1: 54–81.

Gladden, James M., Richard L. Irwin, and William A. Sutton. 2001. "Managing North American Major Professional Sport Teams in the New Millennium: A Focus on Building Brand Equity." *Journal of Sport Management* 15, no. 4: 297–317.

Gladden, James M., George R. Milne, and William A. Sutton. 1998. "A Conceptual Framework for Assessing Brand Equity in Division I College Athletics." *Journal of Sport Management* 12, no. 1: 1–19.

Gordon, Joye, and Susan Berhow. 2009. "University Websites and Dialogic Features for Building Relationships with Potential Sudents." *Public Relations Review* 35, no. 2: 150–52.

Gray, Gordon T., and Stacia Wert-Gray. 2012. "Customer Retention in Sports Organization Marketing: Examining the Impact of Team Identification and Satisfaction with Team Performance." *International Journal of Consumer Studies* 36, no. 3: 275–81.

Greenwood, S., A. Perrin, and M. Duggan. 2016. "Social Media Update 2016." Last Modified November 11, 2016. Retrieved April 8, 2017 from http://www.pewinternet.org/2016/11/11/social-media-update-2016/.

Gronroos, Christian. 1994. "From Marketing Mix to Relationship Marketing: Towards a Paradigm Shift in Marketing." *Asia-Australia Marketing Journal* 2, no. 1: 9–29.

———. 2004. "The Relationship Marketing Process: Communication, Interaction, Dialogue, Value." *Journal of Business & Industrial Marketing* 19, no. 2: 99–113.

Gummerus, Johanna, Veronica Liljander, Emil Weman, and Minna Pihlström. 2012. "Customer Engagement in a Facebook Brand Community." *Management Research Review* 35, no. 9: 857–77.

Hambrick, Marion E., and Sun J. Kang. 2015. "Pin It: Exploring How Professional Sports Organizations Use Pinterest as a Communications and Relationship-Marketing Tool." *Communication & Sport* 3, no. 4: 434–57.

Hambrick, Marion E., and Tara Q. Mahoney. 2011. "'It's Incredible—Trust Me': Exploring the Role of Celebrity Athletes as Marketers in Online Social Networks." *International Journal of Sport Management and Marketing* 10, no. 3–4: 161–79.

Hambrick, Marion E., Jason M. Simmons, Greg P. Greenhalgh, and T. Christopher Greenwell. 2010. "Understanding Professional Athletes' Use of Twitter: A Content Analysis of Athlete Tweets." *International Journal of Sport Communication* 3, no. 4: 454–71.

Haslam, S. Alexander, and Naomi Ellemers. 2005. "Social Identity in Industrial and Organizational Psychology: Concepts, Controversies, and Contributions."

In *International Review of Industrial and Organizational Psychology Vol. 20* by Gerard P. Hodgkinson and J. Kevin Ford, 39–118. West Sussex, UK: John Wiley & Sons, Ltd.

Hausman, Jerry A., and Gregory K. Leonard. 1997. "Superstars in the National Basketball Association: Economic Value and Policy." *Journal of Labor Economics* 15, no. 4: 586–624.

Havard, Cody T. 2014. "Glory Out of Reflected Failure: The Examination of How Rivalry Affects Sport Fans." *Sport Management Review* 17, no. 3: 243–53.

Hedlund, David P. 2014. "Creating Value through Membership and Participation in Sport Fan Consumption Communities." *European Sport Management Quarterly* 14, no. 1: 50–71.

Heine, C. 2016. "Eight Stats That Show How Huge an Opportunity Instagram Is for Marketers." Last Modified September 29, 2016. Retrieved April 8, 2017 from http://www.adweek.com/digital/8-stats-show-how-huge-opportunity-instagram-sports-marketers-173809/.

Heere, Bob. 2010. "A New Approach to Measure Perceived Brand Personality Associations among Consumers." *Sport Marketing Quarterly* 19, no. 1: 17–24.

Heere, Bob, and Geoff Dickson. 2008. "Measuring Attitudinal Loyalty: Separating the Terms of Affective Commitment and Attitudinal Loyalty." *Journal of Sport Management* 22, no. 2: 227–39.

Heere, Bob, and Jeffrey D. James. 2007. "Sports Teams and Their Communities: Examining the Influence of External Group Identities on Team Identity." *Journal of Sport Management* 21, no. 3: 319–37.

Higgins, E. Tory, and Abigail A. Scholer. 2009. "Engaging the Consumer: The Science and Art of the Value Creation Process." *Journal of Consumer Psychology* 19, no. 2: 100–14.

Hogg, Michael A., Deborah J. Terry, and Katherine M. White. 1995. "A Tale of Two Theories: A Critical Comparison of Identity Theory with Social Identity Theory." *Social Psychology Quarterly* 58, no. 4: 255–69.

Hollebeek, Linda D., Mark S. Glynn, and Roderick J. Brodie. 2014. "Consumer Brand Engagement in Social Media: Conceptualization, Scale Development and Validation." *Journal of Interactive Marketing* 28, no. 2: 149–65.

Hopwood, Maria K. 2005. "Public Relations Practice in English County Cricket." *Corporate Communications: An International Journal* 10, no. 3: 201–12.

Horton, Donald, and R. Richard Wohl. 1956. "Mass Communication and Para-Social Interaction: Observations on Intimacy at a Distance." *Psychiatry* 19, no. 3: 215–29.

Ingenhoff, Diana, and A. Martina Koelling. 2009. "The Potential of Web Sites as a Relationship Building Tool for Charitable Fundraising NPOs." *Public Relations Review* 35, no. 1: 66–73.

Ioakimidis, Marilou. 2010. "Online Marketing of Professional Sports Clubs: Engagement Fans on a New Playing Field." *International Journal of Sports Marketing & Sponsorship* 11, no. 4: 2–13.

Islam, Jamid Ul, and Zillur Rahman. 2016. "The Transpiring Journey of Customer Engagement Research in Marketing: A Systematic Review of the Past Decade." *Management Decision* 54, no. 8: 2008–34.

Johnston, Kim A. 2014. "Public Relations and Engagement: Theoretical Imperatives of a Multidimensional Concept." *Journal of Public Relations Research* 26, no. 5: 381–83.

Kang, Chanho. 2015."Development of a Brand Personality Scale in Professional Sports." In poster presented at the annual meeting of the Sport Marketing Association Conference, Atlanta, GA.

Kaplan, Andreas M., and Michael Haenlein. 2010. "Users of the World Unite! The Challenges and Opportunities of Social Media." *Business Horizons*, 53: 59–68.

Kaplan, Andreas M., and Michael Haenlein. 2011a. "The Early Bird Catches the News: Nine Things You Should Know about Micro-Blogging." *Business Horizons* 54, no. 2: 105–13.

Kaplan, Andreas M., and Michael Haenlein. 2011b. "Two Hearts in Three-Quarter Time: How to Waltz the Social Media/Viral Marketing Dance." *Business Horizons* 54, no. 3: 253–63.

Karjaluoto, Heikki, Juha Munnukka, and Milja Salmi. 2016. "How Do Brand Personality, Identification, and Relationship Length Drive Loyalty in Sports?" *Journal of Service Theory and Practice* 26, no. 1: 50–71.

Kassing, Jeffrey W., and Jimmy Sanderson. 2009. ""You're the Kind of Guy that We All Want for a Drinking Buddy": Expressions of Parasocial Interaction on Floydlandis. com." *Western Journal of Communication* 73, no. 2: 182–203.

Kassing, Jeffrey W., and Jimmy Sanderson. 2010. "Fan–Athlete Interaction and Twitter Tweeting through the Giro: A Case Study." *International Journal of Sport Communication* 3, no. 1: 113–28.

Kaynak, Erdener, Gulberk Gultekin Salman, and Ekrem Tatoglu. 2008. "An Integrative Framework Linking Brand Associations and Brand Loyalty in Professional Sports." *Journal of Brand Management* 15, no. 5: 336–57.

Keller, Kevin Lane. 1993. "Conceptualizing, Measuring, and Managing Customer-Based Brand Equity." *The Journal of Marketing* 57, no. 1: 1–22.

Kent, Michael L., and Maureen Taylor. 1998. "Building Dialogic Relationships through the World Wide Web." *Public Relations Review* 24, no. 3: 321–34.

Kent, Michael L., and Maureen Taylor. 2002. "Toward a Dialogic Theory of Public Relations." *Public Relations Review* 28, no. 1: 21–37.

Kerpen, David. 2015. *Likable Social Media: How to Delight Your Customers, Create an Irresistible Brand, and Be Generally Amazing on Facebook (and Other Social Networks).* New York: McGraw-Hill. Kindle.

Khang, Hyoungkoo, Eyun-Jung Ki, and Lan Ye. 2012. "Social Media Research in Advertising, Communication, Marketing, and Public Relations, 1997–2010." *Journalism & Mass Communication Quarterly* 89, no. 2: 279–98.

Kietzmann, Jan H., Kristopher Hermkens, Ian P. McCarthy, and Bruno S. Silvestre. 2011. "Social Media? Get Serious! Understanding the Functional Building Blocks of Social Media." *Business Horizons* 54, no. 3: 241–51.

Kim, Carolyn Mae. 2016. *Social Media Campaigns: Strategies for Public Relations and Marketing.* New York: Routledge. Kindle.

Kim, Young-Ei, Jung-Wan Lee, and Yong-Ki Lee. 2008. "Relationship between Brand Personality and the Personality of Consumers, and Its Application to Corporate Branding Strategy." *Journal of Global Academy of Marketing* 18, no. 3: 27–57.

Kim, Young Do, Marshall Magnusen, and Yukyoum Kim. 2012. "Revisiting Sport Brand Personality: Scale Development and Validation." *Journal of Multidisciplinary Research* 4, no. 3: 65–80.

Kim, Kyeongheui, Jongwon Park, and Jungkeun Kim. 2014. "Consumer–Brand Relationship Quality: When and How It Helps Brand Extensions." *Journal of Business Research* 67, no. 4: 591–97.

Kim, Jihyun, and Hayeon Song. 2016. "Celebrity's Self-Disclosure on Twitter and Parasocial Relationships: A Mediating Role of Social Presence." *Computers in Human Behavior* 62: 570–77.

Kim, Yu Kyoum, and Galen Trail. 2011. "A Conceptual Framework for Understanding Relationships between Sport Consumers and Sport Organizations: A Relationship Quality Approach." *Journal of Sport Management* 25, no. 1: 57–69.

Kohli, Chiranjeev, Rajneesh Suri, and Anuj Kapoor. 2015. "Will Social Media Kill Branding?" *Business Horizons* 58, no. 1: 35–44.

Kristiansen, Elsa, and Antonio S. Williams. 2015. "Communicating the Athlete as a Brand: An Examination of LPGA Star Suzann Pettersen." *International Journal of Sport Communication* 8, no. 3: 371–88.

Kunkel, Thilo, Jason P. Doyle, and Daniel C. Funk. 2014. "Exploring Sport Brand Development Strategies to Strengthen Consumer Involvement with the Product—The Case of the Australian A-League." *Sport Management Review* 17, no. 4: 470–83.

Kwon, Eun Sook, and Yongjun Sung. 2011. "Follow Me! Global Marketers' Twitter Use." *Journal of Interactive Advertising* 12, no. 1: 4–16.

Labrecque, Lauren I. 2014. "Fostering Consumer–Brand Relationships in Social Media Environments: The Role of Parasocial Interaction." *Journal of Interactive Marketing* 28, no. 2: 134–48.

Lee, Jason W., Kimberly S. Miloch, Patrick Kraft, and Lance Tatum. 2008. "Building the Brand: A Case Study of Troy University." *Sport Marketing Quarterly* 17, no. 3: 178–82.

L'Etang, Jacquie. 2006. "Public Relations and Sport in Promotional Culture." *Public Relations Review* 32, no. 4: 386–94.

Levenshus, Abbey. 2010. "Online Relationship Management in a Presidential Campaign: A Case Study of the Obama Campaign's Management of Its Internet-Integrated Grassroots Effort." *Journal of Public Relations Research* 22, no. 3: 313–35.

Lindlof, Thomas R., and Bryan C. Taylor. 2011. *Qualitative Communication Research Methods* (3rd ed.). Los Angeles, CA: Sage.

Linvill, Darren L., Sara E. McGee, and Laura K. Hicks. 2012. "Colleges' and Universities' Use of Twitter: A Content Analysis." *Public Relations Review* 38, no. 4: 636–38.

Lock, Daniel, Tracy Taylor, Daniel Funk, and Simon Darcy. 2012. "Exploring the Development of Team Identification." *Journal of Sport Management* 26, no. 4: 283–94.

Lovejoy, Kristen, Richard D. Waters, and Gregory D. Saxton. 2012. "Engaging Stakeholders through Twitter: How Nonprofit Organizations Are Getting More out of 140 Characters or Less." *Public Relations Review* 38, no. 2: 313–18.

Low, George S., and Charles W. Lamb Jr. 2000. "The Measurement and Dimensionality of Brand Associations." *Journal of Product & Brand Management* 9, no. 6: 350–70.

Lutrell, Regina. 2014. *Social Media: How to Engage, Share, and Connect.* London: Rowman & Littlefield.

Madrigal, Robert, and Johnny Chen. 2008. "Moderating and Mediating Effects of Team Identification in Regard to Causal Attributions and Summary Judgments Following a Game Outcome." *Journal of Sport Management* 22, no. 6: 717–33.

Magrath, Victoria, and Helen McCormick. 2013. "Branding Design Elements of Mobile Fashion Retail Apps." *Journal of Fashion Marketing and Management: An International Journal* 17, no. 1: 98–114.

Mahan, J. E., and Stephen R. McDaniel. 2006. "The New Online Arena: Sport, Marketing, and Media Converge in Cyberspace." In *Handbook of Sports and Media*, edited by Arthur A. Raney and Jennings Bryant, 409–31. New York: Routledge.

Mahony, Daniel F., Robert Madrigal, and Dennis Howard. 2000. "Using the Psychological Commitment to Team (PCT) Scale to Segment Sport Consumers Based on Loyalty." *Sport Marketing Quarterly* 9, no. 1: 15–25.

Malthouse, Edward C., Bobby J. Calder, Su Jung Kim, and Mark Vandenbosch. 2016. "Evidence That User-Generated Content That Produces Engagement Increases Purchase Behaviours." *Journal of Marketing Management* 32, no. 5–6: 427–44.

Mangold, W. Glynn, and David J. Faulds. 2009. "Social Media: The New Hybrid Element of the Promotion Mix." *Business Horizons* 52, no. 4: 357–65.McAllister-Spooner, Sheila M., and Michael L. Kent. 2009. "Dialogic Public Relations and Resource Dependency: New Jersey Community Colleges as Models for Web Site Effectiveness." *Atlantic Journal of Communication* 17, no. 4: 220–39.

McCrae, Robert R., and Paul T. Costa. 1995. "Trait Explanations in Personality Psychology." *European Journal of Personality* 9, no. 4: 231–52.

McGowan, Richard A., and J. F. Mahon. 2009. "Corporate Social Responsibility in Professional Sports: An Analysis of the NBA, NFL, and MLB." *Academy of Business Disciplines Journal* 1, no. 1: 45–82.

McNely, Brian J. 2012. "Shaping Organizational Image-Power through Images: Case Histories of Instagram." In *Professional Communication Conference (IPCC), 2012 IEEE International*, pp. 1–8.

MediaPostNEWS. Retrieved June 16, 2013, from Sports Fans Big Fans of Mobile: http://www.mediapost.com/publications/article/191618/.

Men, Linjuan Rita, and Wan-Hsiu Sunny Tsai. 2014. "Perceptual, Attitudinal, and Behavioral Outcomes of Organization–Public Engagement on Corporate Social Networking Sites." *Journal of Public Relations Research* 26, no. 5: 417–35.

Meng, Matthew D., Constantino Stavros, and Kate Westberg. 2015. "Engaging Fans through Social Media: Implications for Team Identification." *Sport, Business and Management: An International Journal* 5, no. 3: 199–217.

Morgan-Thomas, Anna, and Cleopatra Veloutsou. 2013. "Beyond Technology Acceptance: Brand Relationships and Online Brand Experience." *Journal of Business Research* 66, no. 1: 21–27.

Moyer, Caitlin, Jim Pokrywczynski, and Robert J. Griffin. 2015. "The Relationship of Fans' Sports-Team Identification and Facebook Usage to Purchase of Team Products." *Journal of Sports Media* 10, no. 1: 31–49.

Muntinga, Daniel G., Marjolein Moorman, and Edith G. Smit. 2011. "Introducing COBRAs: Exploring Motivations for Brand-Related Social Media Use." *International Journal of Advertising* 30, no. 1: 13–46.

Newport, K. 2017. "NBA, Twitter Unveil Team Hashtags, Emojis for 2016–17 Season. Last Modified February 16, 2017. Retrieved February 24, 2017 from http://bleacherreport.com/articles/2671553-nba-twitter-unveil-team-hashtags-emojis-for-2016–17-seasonl.

Nobre, Helena M., Kip Becker, and Carlos Brito. 2010. "Brand Relationships: A Personality-Based Approach." *Journal of Service Science and Management* 3, no. 2: 206–17.

Owen, William Foster. 1984. "Interpretive Themes in Relational Communication." *The Quarterly Journal of Speech* 70, no. 3: 274–86.

Page, Ruth. 2012. "The Lingusitics of Self-Branding and Miro-Celebrity in Twitter Hashtags." *Discourse & Communication* 6, no. 2: 181–201.

Park, Hyojung, and Bryan H. Reber. 2008. "Relationship Building and the Use of Web Sites: How Fortune 500 Corporations Use Their Web Sites to Build Relationships." *Public Relations Review* 34, no. 4: 409–11.

Patterson, Maurice. 1999. "Re-Appraising the Concept of Brand Image." *Journal of Brand Management* 6: 409–36.

Pedersen, Paul M., Kimberly S. Miloch, and Pamela C. Laucella. 2007. *Strategic Sport Communication.* Champaign, IL: Human Kinetics.

Pegoraro, Ann. 2010. "Look Who's Talking—Athletes on Twitter: A Case Study." *International Journal of Sport Communication* 3, no. 4: 501–14.

———. 2014. "Sport Fandom in the Digital World." In *Routledge Handbook of Sport Communication*, edited by P. M. Pedersen, 248–58. New York: Routledge.

Pegoraro, Ann, and Naila Jinnah. 2012. "Tweet'em and Reap'em: The Impact of Professional Athletes' Use of Twitter on Current and Potential Sponsorship Opportunities." *Journal of Brand Strategy* 1, no. 1: 85–97.

Perse, Elizabeth M., and Rebecca B. Rubin. 1989. "Attribution in Social and Parasocial Relationships." *Communication Research* 16, no. 1: 59–77.

Phillips, Barbara J., Edward F. McQuarrie, and W. Glenn Griffin. 2014. "The Face of the Brand: How Art Directors Understand Visual Brand Identity." *Journal of Advertising* 43, no. 4: 318–32.

Phua, Joe J. 2010. "Sports Fans and Media Use: Influence on Sports Fan Identification and Collective Self-Esteem." *International Journal of Sport Communication* 3, no. 2: 190–206.

Plummer, Joseph T. 2000. "How Personality Makes a Difference." *Journal of Advertising Research* 40, no. 6: 79–83.

Pronschinske, Mya, Mark D. Groza, and Matthew Walker. 2012. "Attracting Facebook 'Fans': The Importance of Authenticity and Engagement as a Social Networking Strategy for Professional Sport Teams." *Sport Marketing Quarterly* 21, no. 4: 221–31

Rapaport, Daniel. "Couple Who Met at Hawks' Tinder Night Get Married on Court." SI.com. March 06, 2018. Accessed June 15, 2018. https://www.si.com/nba/2018/03/06/atlanta-hawks-tinder-night-swipe-right-couple-married.

Richelieu, Andre, and Frank Pons. 2009. "If Brand Equity Matters, Where Is the Brand Strategy? A Look at Canadian Hockey Teams in the NHL." *International Journal of Sport Management and Marketing* 5, no. 1–2: 162–82.

Ross, Stephen D. 2006. "A Conceptual Framework for Understanding Spectator-Based Brand Equity." *Journal of Sport Management* 20, no. 1: 22–38.

———. 2008. "Assessing the Use of the Brand Personality Scale in Team Sport." *International Journal of Sport Management and Marketing* 3, no. 1–2: 23–38.

Ross, Stephen D., Jeffrey D. James, and Patrick Vargas. 2006. "Development of a Scale to M Measure Team Brand Associations in Professional Sport." *Journal of Sport Management* 20, no. 2: 260–79.

Rubin, Alan M., Elizabeth M. Perse, and Robert A. Powell. 1985. "Loneliness, Parasocial Interaction, and Local Television News Viewing." *Human Communication Research* 12, no. 2: 155–80.

Rybalko, Svetlana, and Trent Seltzer. 2010. "Dialogic Communication in 140 Characters or Less: How Fortune 500 Companies Engage Stakeholders Using Twitter." *Public Relations Review* 36, no. 4: 336–41.

Saffer, Adam J., Erich J. Sommerfeldt, and Maureen Taylor. 2013. "The Effects of Organizational Twitter Interactivity on Organization–Public Relationships." *Public Relations Review* 39, no. 3: 213–15.

Salomon, Danielle. 2013. "Moving on from Facebook: Using Instagram to Connect with Undergraduates and Engage in Teaching and Learning." *College & Research Libraries News* 74, no. 8: 408–12.

Sanderson, J., and J. W. Kassing. 2014. "New Media and the Evolution of Fan-Athlete Interaction." In *Routledge Handbook of Sport and New Media*, edited by A. C. Billings and M. Hardin, 247–58. New York: Routledge.

Sanderson, Jimmy. 2008a. "Spreading the Word: Emphatic Interaction Displays on Blogmaverick.com." *Journal of Media Psychology: Theories, Methods, and Applications* 20, no. 4: 156–67.

———. 2008b. "You are the Type of Person that Children Should Look Up to as a Hero": Parasocial Interaction on 38pitches.com." *International Journal of Sport Communication* 1, no. 3: 337–60.

Sarconi, P. 2017. "Why Instagram Is Suddenly the Place for Sports Highlights." Last modified March 16, 2017. Retrieved April 08, 2017 from https://www.wired.com/2017/03/instagram-sports-highlights/.

Schade, Michael, Rico Piehler, and Christoph Burmann. 2014. "Sport Club Brand Personality Scale (SCBPS): A New Brand Personality Scale for Sport Clubs." *Journal of Brand Management* 21, no. 7–8: 650–63.

Schivinski, Bruno, George Christodoulides, and Dariusz Dabrowski. 2016. "Measuring Consumers' Engagement with Brand-Related Social-Media Content." *Journal of Advertising Research* 56, no. 1: 64–80.

Schwartz, N. 2016. "How to Use Twitter Emojis for All 32 NFL Teams." Last modified October 20, 2016. Accessed February 24, 2017, from http://www.foxsports.com/nfl/gallery/how-to-use-nfl-team-twitter-emojis-hashtags-090716.

Seltzer, Trent, and Michael A. Mitrook. 2007. "The Dialogic Potential of Weblogs in Relationship Building." *Public Relations Review* 33, no. 2: 227–29.

Seo, Won Jae, and B. Christine Green. 2008. "Development of the Motivation Scale for Sport Online Consumption." *Journal of Sport Management* 22, no. 1: 82–109.

Shani, David. 1997. "A Framework for Implementing Relationship Marketing in the Sport Industry." *Sport Marketing Quarterly* 6: 9–16.

Sheth, Jagdish N. 2002. "The Future of Relationship Marketing." *Journal of Services Marketing* 16, no. 7: 590–92.

Simmons, Geoffrey J. 2007. "'i-Branding': Developing the Internet as a Branding Tool." *Marketing Intelligence & Planning* 25, no. 6: 544–62.

Smith, Brian G. 2010. "Socially Distributing Public Relations: Twitter, Haiti, and Interactivity in Social Media." *Public Relations Review* 36, no. 4: 329–35.

Smith, Lauren Reichart, and Jimmy Sanderson. 2015. "I'm Going to Instagram it! An Analysis of Athlete Self-Presentation on Instagram." *Journal of Broadcasting & Electronic Media* 59, no. 2: 342–58.

Smith, Lauren Reichart, and Kenny D. Smith. 2012. "Identity in Twitter's Hashtag Culture: A Sport-Media-Consumption Case Study." *International Journal of Sport Communication* 5, no. 4: 539–57.

Smith, Aaron CT, and Hans M. Westerbeek. 2007. "Sport as a Vehicle for Deploying Corporate Social Responsibility." *Journal of Corporate Citizenship* 25, no. 1: 43–54.

"Sports Illustrated Social 100." Sports Illustrated: Social 100. Accessed June 22, 2017. http://www.si.com/specials/social-100-2015/#two.

Statista. 2018. "Top U.S. Mobile Social Apps by Users 2018 | Statistic." Accessed June 1, 2018. https://www.statista.com/statistics/248074/most-popular-us-social-networking-apps-ranked-by-audience/.

Stavros, Constantino, Matthew D. Meng, Kate Westberg, and Francis Farrelly. 2014. "Understanding Fan Motivation for Interacting on Social Media." *Sport Management Review* 17, no. 4: 455–69.

Stavros, Constantino, Nigel K. Li Pope, and Hume Winzar. 2008. "Relationship Marketing in Australian Professional Sport: An Extension of the Shani Famework." *Sport Marketing Quarterly* 17, no. 3: 135–45.

Stavros, Constantino, and Kate Westberg. 2009. "Using Triangulation and Multiple Case Studies to Advance Relationship Marketing Theory." *Qualitative Market Research: An International Journal* 12, no. 3: 307–20.

Stets, Jan E., and Peter J. Burke. 2000. "Identity Theory and Social Identity Theory." *Social Psychology Quarterly* 63 no. 3: 224–37.

Stevens, Shawn, and Philip J. Rosenberger. 2012. "The Influence of Involvement, Following Sport and Fan Identification on Fan Loyalty: An Australian Perspective." *International Journal of Sports Marketing and Sponsorship* 13, no. 3: 57–71.

Stever, Gayle S., and Kevin Lawson. 2013. "Twitter as a Way for Celebrities to Communicate with Fans: Implications for the Study of Parasocial Interaction." *North American Journal of Psychology* 15, no. 2: 339–54.

Stewart, Bob, Aaron Smith, and Matthew Nicholson. 2003. "Sport Consumer Typologies: A Critical Review." *Sport Marketing Quarterly* 12, no. 4: 206–16.

Strauss, Anselm, and Juliet Corbin. 1998. *Basics of Qualitative Research: Techniques and Procedures for Developing Grounded Theory.* Thousand Oaks, CA: Sage.

Summers, Jane, and Melissa Johnson Morgan. 2008. "More Than Just the Media: Considering the Role of Public Relations in the Creation of Sporting Celebrity and the Management of Fan Expectations." *Public Relations Review* 34, no. 2: 176–82.

Sun, Tao. 2010. "Antecedents and Consequences of Parasocial Interaction with Sport Athletes and Identification with Sport Teams." *Journal of Sport Behavior* 33, no. 2: 194–217.

Sun, Tao, and Guohua Wu. 2012. "Influence of Personality Traits on Parasocial Relationship with Sports Celebrities: A Hierarchical Approach." *Journal of Consumer Behaviour* 11, no. 2: 136–46.

Sutton, William A., Mark A. McDonald, George R. Milne, and John Cimperman. 1997. "Creating and Fostering Fan Identification in Professional Sports." *Sport Marketing Quarterly* 6: 15–22.

Swaminathan, Vanitha, Karen M. Stilley, and Rohini Ahluwalia. 2008. "When Brand Personality Matters: The Moderating Role of Attachment Styles." *Journal of Consumer Research* 35, no. 6: 985–1002.

Sweetser, Kaye D., and Ruthann Weaver Lariscy. 2008. "Candidates Make Good Friends: An Analysis of Candidates' Uses of Facebook." *International Journal of Strategic Communication* 2, no. 3: 175–98.

Tajfel, Henri. 1982. "Social Psychology of Intergroup Relations." *Annual Review of Psychology* 33, no. 1: 1–39.

Tajfel, Henri, and John C. Turner. 2004. "The Social Identity Theory of Intergroup Behavior." In *Political Psychology: Key Readings.* Edited by John T. Jost and Jim Sidanius, 367–90. New York: Psychology Press.

Taylor, Maureen, and Michael L. Kent. 2004. "Congressional Web Sites and Their Potential for Public Dialogue." *Atlantic Journal of Communication* 12, no. 2: 59–76.

Taylor, Maureen, and Michael L. Kent. 2014. "Dialogic Engagement: Clarifying Foundational Concepts." *Journal of Public Relations Research* 26, no. 5: 384–98.

TEDxTalks. "Using Sports for Social Change | Andrew Billings | TEDxBirminghamSalon." YouTube. October 09, 2014. Accessed May 15, 2018. https://www.youtube.com/watch?v=xfjZ-tWFxpA.

"The Complete History of Instagram." Visual.ly. October 06, 2014. Accessed September 25, 2015. https://visual.ly/community/infographic/complete-history-instagram.

Thomson, Matthew. 2006. "Human Brands: Investigating Antecedents to Consumers' Strong Attachments to Celebrities." *Journal of Marketing* 70, no. 3: 104–19.

Thompson, Ashleigh-Jane, Andrew J. Martin, Sarah Gee, and Andrea N. Eagleman. 2014. "Examining the Development of a Social Media Strategy for a National Sport Organisation: A Case Study of Tennis New Zealand." *Journal of Applied Sport Management* 6, no. 2: 42–63.

Trepte, Sabine. 2006. "Social Identity Theory." In *Psychology of Entertainment*, 255–71 New York: Routledge.

Tsai, Shu-pei. 2011. "Strategic Relationship Management and Service Brand Marketing." *European Journal of Marketing* 45, no. 7/8: 1194–1213.

Tsiotsou, Rodoula. 2012. "Developing a Scale for Measuring the Personality of Sport Teams." *Journal of Services Marketing* 26, no. 4: 238–52.

Tuškej, Urška, Urša Golob, and Klement Podnar. 2013. "The Role of Consumer–Brand Identification in Building Brand Relationships." *Journal of Business Research* 66, no. 1: 53–59.

Urban, Jeff. "Millennial Sports Fans Win: 3 Stats That Prove Social Sports Is Where The Game Is." June 17, 2016. Accessed March 4, 2018. https://www.mediapost.com/publications/article/278343/millennial-sports-fans-win-3-stats-that-prove-soc.html.

Underwood, Robert, Edward Bond, and Robert Baer. 2001. "Building Service Brands via Social Identity: Lessons from the Sports Marketplace." *Journal of Marketing Theory and Practice* 9, no. 1: 1–13.

Van Doorn, Jenny, Katherine N. Lemon, Vikas Mittal, Stephan Nass, Doreén Pick, Peter Pirner, and Peter C. Verhoef. 2010. "Customer Engagement Behavior: Theoretical Foundations and Research Directions." *Journal of Service Research* 13, no. 3: 253–66.

Vivek, Shiri D., Sharon E. Beatty, and Robert M. Morgan. 2012. "Customer Engagement: Exploring Customer Relationships beyond Purchase." *Journal of Marketing Theory and Practice* 20, no. 2: 122–46.

Wallace, Laci, Jacquelyn Wilson, and Kimberly Miloch. 2011. "Sporting Facebook: A Content Analysis of NCAA Organizational Sport Pages and Big 12 Conference Athletic Department Pages." *International Journal of Sport Communication* 4, no. 4: 422–44.

Walsh, Patrick, Galen Clavio, M. David Lovell, and Matthew Blaszka. 2013. "Differences in Event Brand Personality between Social Media Users and Non-Users." *Sport Marketing Quarterly* 22, no. 4: 214–23.

Wann, Daniel L. 1995. "Preliminary Validation of the Sport Fan Motivation Scale." *Journal of Sport and Social Issues* 19, no. 4: 377–96.

———. 2006. "Understanding the Positive Social Psychological Benefits of Sport Team Identification: The Team Identification-Social Psychological Health Model." *Group Dynamics: Theory, Research, and Practice* 10, no. 4: 272–96.

Wann, Daniel L., and Nyla R. Branscombe. 1993. "Sport Fans: Measuring Degree of Identification with Their Team." *International Journal of Sport Psychology* 24, no. 1: 1–17.

Waters, Richard D., Emily Burnett, Anna Lamm, and Jessica Lucas. 2009. "Engaging Stakeholders Through Social Networking: How Nonprofit Organizations Are Using Facebook." *Public Relations Review* 35, no. 2: 102–6.

Waters, Richard D., Rachel R. Canfield, Jenny M. Foster, and Eva E. Hardy. 2011. "Applying the Dialogic Theory to Social Networking Sites: Examining How University Health Centers Convey Health Messages on Facebook." *Journal of Social Marketing* 1, no. 3: 211–27.

Waters, Richard D., and Justin Walden. 2015. "Charting Fandom through Social Media Communication: A Multi-League Analysis of Professional Sports Teams' Facebook Content." *Prism,* 12 no. 1: 1–18.

Waters, Richard D., and Jensen M. Williams. 2011. "Squawking, Tweeting, Cooing, and Hooting: Analyzing the Communication Patterns of Government Agencies on Twitter." *Journal of Public Affairs* 11, no. 4: 353–63.

Watkins, Brandi A. 2014a. "Revisiting the Social Identity–Brand Equity Model: An Application to Professional Sports." *Journal of Sport Management* 28, no. 4: 471–80.

———. 2014b. "Social Identification and Social Media in Sports: Implications for Sport Brands." In *Routledge Handbook of Sport and New Media*, edited by A. C. Billings and M. Hardin, 200–10. New York: Routledge.

———. 2016. "Extending the Conversation: Audience Reactions to Dialogic Activity on Twitter." In *Public Relations and Participatory Culture: Fandom, Social Media, and Community Engagement*, edited by Natalie Tindall and Amber Hutchins, 33–44. New York: Routledge.

Watkins, Brandi A. 2017. "Experimenting with Dialogue on Twitter: An Examination of the Influence of the Dialogic Principles on Engagement, Interaction, and Attitude." *Public Relations Review* 43, no. 1 (2017): 163–71.

Watkins, Brandi A., and William J. Gonzenbach. 2013. "Assessing University Brand Personality Through Logos: An Analysis of the Use of Academics and Athletics in University Branding." *Journal of Marketing for Higher Education* 23, no. 1: 15–33.

Watkins, Brandi, and Jason W. Lee. 2016. "Communicating Brand Identity on Social Media: A Case Study of the Use of Instagram and Twitter for Collegiate Athletic Branding." *International Journal of Sport Communication* 9, no. 4 (2016): 476–98.

Watkins, Brandi, and Regina Lewis. 2014a. "Winning with Apps: A Case Study of the Current Branding Strategies Employed on Professional Sport Teams' Mobile Apps." *International Journal of Sport Communication* 7, no. 3 (2014): 399–416.

———. 2014b. "Initiating Dialogue on Social Media: An Investigation of Athletes' Use of Dialogic Principles and Structural Features of Twitter." *Public Relations Review* 40, no. 5: 853–55.

Williams, Jo, and Susan J. Chinn. 2010. "Meeting Relationship-Marketing Goals Through Social Media: A Conceptual Model for Sport Marketers." *International Journal of Sport Communication* 3, no. 4: 422–37.

Williams, Antonio S., DaeYeon Kim, Kwame Agyemang, and Tywan G. Martin. 2015. "All Brands Are Not Created Equal: Understanding the Role of Athletes in Sport-Brand Architecture." *Journal of Multidisciplinary Research* 7, no. 3: 75–86.

Xie, Lexing, Apostol Natsev, John R. Kender, Matthew Hill, and John R. Smith. 2011. "Visual Memes in Social Media: Tracking Real-World News in YouTube Videos." In *Proceedings of the 19th ACM international conference on Multimedia*, pp. 53–62. ACM, 2011.

Index

About the Author

Brandi Watkins, PhD (The University of Alabama), is an assistant professor of public relations in the Department of Communication at Virginia Tech. Her research focuses on how organizations use social media to build, enhance, and maintain relationships with key stakeholder groups. Her work has been published in *Public* Relations *Review*, *Journal of Brand Management*, *Journal of Social Media and Society,* and *International Journal of Sport Communication*. At Virginia Tech, she teaches classes in public relations and social media.

Lightning Source UK Ltd.
Milton Keynes UK
UKHW021840041020
370982UK00017B/390